"As a parent, I feel Lynn's book is an essential guide and support for anyone concerned about their son's or daughter's eating habits, self-esteem and general wellbeing."
Bobby Davro – entertainer

"Men Get Eating Disorders Too fully supports Hope With Eating Disorders. As an issue so often associated with women, we are pleased the specific and unique needs of men are recognised in this fantastic book."
Men Get Eating Disorders Too (mengetedstoo.co.uk)

"As a former sufferer myself of what is still considered a bit of a taboo subject, I found this book delivers information in a friendly, easy to understand way, making you want to read on."
Suzanne Dando, Olympic gymnast

"Lynn's passion and determination to help people whose lives are affected by eating disorders is inspiring."
Jo Swinson, MP

"I support Lynn with her book as it will make people more aware of eating disorders and the impact they have, not only on the person directly affected but also their family and friends."
John Stapleton, television presenter

"I am so pleased to have contributed to a book with such a positive and inspiring message."
Nicki Waterman, fitness expert

"Now and again you meet someone special. Someone whose care and generosity sets out to make a genuine difference. Lynn is one such person."
Steve Blacknell, broadcaster/media advisor

"So often, we are approached by people concerned about a son or daughter, friend or colleague with an eating disorder, asking us what they can do. Now, finally we have an answer for them – read this book!"
Ruth Rogers and Natasha Devon, Co-directors – Body Gossip

D1392350

Hope
with EATING
DISORDERS

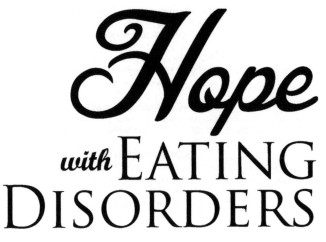

Hope
with EATING DISORDERS

A self-help guide for parents, carers
and friends of sufferers

LYNN CRILLY

INSIGHTS

Australia • Canada • Hong Kong • India
South Africa • United Kingdom • United States

First published and distributed in the United Kingdom by:
Hay House UK Ltd, 292B Kensal Rd, London W10 5BE. Tel.: (44) 20 8962 1230;
Fax: (44) 20 8962 1239. www.hayhouse.co.uk

Published and distributed in the United States of America by:
Hay House, Inc., PO Box 5100, Carlsbad, CA 92018-5100. Tel.: (1) 760 431 7695 or (800) 654 5126;
Fax: (1) 760 431 6948 or (800) 650 5115. www.hayhouse.com

Published and distributed in Australia by:
Hay House Australia Ltd, 18/36 Ralph St, Alexandria NSW 2015. Tel.: (61) 2 9669 4299;
Fax: (61) 2 9669 4144. www.hayhouse.com.au

Published and distributed in the Republic of South Africa by:
Hay House SA (Pty), Ltd, PO Box 990, Witkoppen 2068. Tel./Fax: (27) 11 467 8904.
www.hayhouse.co.za

Published and distributed in India by:
Hay House Publishers India, Muskaan Complex, Plot No.3, B-2, Vasant Kunj, New Delhi – 110 070.
Tel.: (91) 11 4176 1620; Fax: (91) 11 4176 1630. www.hayhouse.co.in

Distributed in Canada by:
Raincoast, 9050 Shaughnessy St, Vancouver, BC V6P 6E5. Tel.: (1) 604 323 7100;
Fax: (1) 604 323 2600

© Lynn Crilly 2012

The moral rights of the author have been asserted.

All rights reserved. No part of this book may be reproduced by any mechanical, photographic or
electronic process, or in the form of a phonographic recording; nor may it be stored in a retrieval
system, transmitted or otherwise be copied for public or private use, other than for 'fair use' as brief
quotations embodied in articles and reviews, without prior written permission of the publisher.

The author of this book does not dispense medical advice or prescribe the use of any technique as a
form of treatment for physical or medical problems without the advice of a physician, either directly or
indirectly. The intent of the author is only to offer information of a general nature to help you in your
quest for emotional and spiritual wellbeing. In the event you use any of the information in this book
for yourself, which is your constitutional right, the author and the publisher assume no responsibility
for your actions.

A catalogue record for this book is available from the British Library.

ISBN 978-1-84850-892-7

Printed and bound in Great Britain by CPI Group (UK) Ltd, Croydon, CR0 4YY

This book is dedicated to...

the memory of my Aunty Babs: thank you for giving me the strength to start writing this book,

AND to my wonderful husband Kevin and our beautiful daughters Charlotte and Samantha for giving me the strength to finish it!

CONTENTS

Contents

ACKNOWLEDGEMENTS

First and foremost I would like to say a big thank you to my husband Kevin, who has always given me his unconditional love and support. His unquestioning belief in me has given me the strength to achieve everything I have so far ... I love you more now than ever before! To our beautiful twin daughters Charlotte and Samantha, I am very proud of the gorgeous young ladies you have become, and love you both very much. Mum and dad, you have always been there for me with your constant love and support. Thank you to my brother Steve and my sister-in-law Sue.

A warm thank you to Kate, Wendy, Jilly, Gerry, Jill, Leanne, Hannah and all my wonderful friends for your unconditional friendship, love and support throughout the years – it means everything to me to know you are always there.

Special thanks go to our GP John Dalzell, who has always given us as a family and me as a professional his unquestioning support. To all the staff at Hinchley Wood Secondary School, for everything you did not only for Sam but Charlotte and the family, too ... thank you!

Thank you to all my clients, both past and present, who have put their trust and belief in me and my work, which has enabled me to help and support them to make the positive changes needed in their lives and, in doing so, changing mine too.

Acknowledgements

Kyra, you have to be one of my biggest supporters ... thank you.

Professor Janet Treasure, who has always actively encouraged me within my role as an eating disorder counsellor, and supported me in every way possible ... thank you so much.

Thank you to my friend Bobby Davro for always encouraging and believing in me.

A special mention to Zowie Edwards, who joined me halfway through my journey of writing this book and helped me through to the end. Thank you for your time, love and patience.

Thank you to my good friend Andy and his fantastic team at DDM Marketing.

I have been privileged to have been supported by so many wonderful people in and out of the public eye, who have all trusted and believed in me enough to make a contribution to my book. I thank you from the bottom of my heart because, without you guys, I would not have a book!

Lastly, thank you to Max Kirsten for encouraging me to approach Carolyn Thorne and the team at Hay House Publishing who, as promised, have given me their professional guidance and support in a very sensitive and caring way.

Thank you to them and indeed again to everyone mentioned above, and all the other people who have helped and supported me along the way. Without you all, I know I would not be who and where I am today, and certainly would never have been in a position to write this book.

FOREWORD

Working with people with eating disorders for over 30 years in order to understand the illness and to help on the way to recovery, I have often heard that one of the most important things that carers can do is maintain hope. This book encapsulates the essence of how hope can be generated and sustained. Hope can be built on understanding more about the illness, building resilience in young people and their families to withstand some of the pressures that can adversely shape development, and increasing trust that recovery is attainable.

A junior doctor described her 12-year illness in a Personal View to the *British Medical Journal*. She said she could summarize her illness in one word: 'isolation'. Although numerous paths lead to isolation, including biological and psychological factors, social factors are of key importance. The noxious influence of shame and stigma drives the individual, and their family, too, into a secret cell of loneliness bereft of the social glue of shared eating and connection.

Lynn demonstrates what can be attained through curiosity and an open mind, and the refusal to accept stigma and secrecy. This book contains the lived experience of diverse forms of eating disorders and glimpses into the variety of ways in which recovery can be attained. Connecting with others with love and respect is key, and this book demonstrates how this can be done.

Professor Janet Treasure PhD FRCP FRCPsych

INTRODUCTION

Carers of eating disorder sufferers feel isolated, lonely, desperate, frustrated, angry and confused. I know this because I was one.

When my beautiful daughter Samantha became anorexic aged just 13 years old, I felt all of the above and more. However, during this time it never occurred to me that I would not be able to find the right help she needed to get better, or the lengths I would have to go to in order to do so. Over the next two years, as the anorexia took hold of Sam's mind and body, it dominated not only her life but the lives of myself, my husband and Sam's twin sister Charlotte, with terrifying rapidity.

My family and I sought many different solutions, desperately looking for the answers to Sam's illness in the private and NHS sectors – all to no avail. Some of the treatments we tried actually made her worse. Sam was slowly disappearing before our eyes; we were losing her and we had seemingly exhausted all the options available to us. My once happy family was now falling apart around me.

I had been told that as her mother I was too close to the situation to have any practical use. As parents, it had been suggested that Sam's condition was in some way our fault (or even her sister Charlotte's).

Something drastic had to happen for us to have any hope of surviving this evil illness. I could not just sit back and reconcile us to our collective fate, as it appeared at the time.

I made the decision to ignore these destructive messages and to rehabilitate Sam myself.

Perhaps a little unorthodox, but it was the start of what was to be the best decision I could possibly have made.

Over the next few months, I injected positive thinking, lots of love and, crucially, hope into what had seemed a hopeless situation. I showed Sam a life outside her eating disorder.

Sam is now healthy and happy, and enjoying life. As a family we worked together to bring Samantha back to life (and back to us), and feel we are now closer than ever for doing so.

I will never forget the bleak times I faced as a mother, watching my daughter waste away, and how futile and frustrated I felt. These feelings are very often echoed in the faces of the carers I now work alongside, in my newfound career as a counsellor. One of my clients suggested to me that I should share my knowledge, my first-hand experience and, most of all, my passion to help others, with other carers and loved ones of people suffering from eating disorders. So I decided to write this book, to help you realize that you are not alone, and that there are answers and solutions to the issues you are facing.

Most important of all, this book will show you that there is *hope*: eating disorders can be beaten, full and lasting recovery is possible, relationships and families can be rebuilt.

Over the pages that follow you will share the experiences of other carers, and realize that the emotions you may be experiencing are normal and natural. You will be given an insight into how your loved one is thinking and feeling, to provide you with a genuine understanding of their condition. All these contributors are real people, but some have had their names changed to protect their identity.

This book also offers a comprehensive guide to all the various treatments available, to help you ascertain which one is most suited to your situation. The book features interviews with some of the world's leading experts in eating disorder research and treatment, and some of the leading organizations in body image, to guide you in the pioneering work that is being done not only to raise awareness but also to make a difference to all concerned.

I have been very privileged to have been supported by over 200 contributors. These range from carers, sufferers, therapists, experts, MPs, celebrities, campaigners and charities, all of whom believe in me and the message my book is giving to you, its reader.

This book emphasizes that each eating disorder sufferer is individual and unique. There is no 'right' or 'wrong' path to recovery. My own experience demonstrates that each family or support network must take whatever action is right for them. If one option proves ineffective, try another – never buy into the myth that eating disorders are incurable. Never give up hope and never give up trying.

You will not find blame, negativity or self-pity within the pages of this book. What you will find is the knowledge to enable you to find the strength and hope you will need to fight and win against these sometimes totally misunderstood illnesses.

Hope and belief are the most fundamental aims of my writing. Hope and belief are crucial in any eating disorder recovery. Hope and belief are essential for both the carers and sufferers alike, not only to enable them to work together, but to help them believe that through communication, understanding, hope and unconditional love, everyone can look forward to a future free from eating disorders.

There are several organizations working tirelessly to raise awareness of the plight of the millions of people worldwide afflicted with eating disorders. I applaud their work in changing attitudes, challenging the stigma and giving support to those concerned. Yet there are relatively few groups dedicated to providing support for the families, carers, colleagues and friends of eating disorder sufferers. Eating disorders are debilitating for everyone who encounters them. The illness permeates every area of the sufferer's life and the lives of their loved ones. The condition of the patient becomes the central focus, which in turn can have devastating consequences for the carers themselves.

Having experienced first-hand some of what you are going through, my main aim in writing this book is to relieve you of some of the burden, confusion and pain you may be feeling, and give you as much knowledge, comfort and strength as I can, to enable you to continue and finish your journey successfully.

Lots of love and *hope* to you, the reader.

Lynn

DONATION

A donation from the proceeds of this book will go to Body Gossip, a campaign which champions natural, healthy and realistic beauty.

Body Gossip takes real-body stories from the public, on a variety of body-related topics, and has a selection of these performed by a cast of celebrities, both in live events and in short films which are put on YouTube (www.youtube.com/bodygossip). In doing so, Body Gossip empowers real people and enables real stories to be told in a high-profile forum, raising awareness and providing support and inspiration to people throughout the globe. Half of the donation made from this book will help Body Gossip to make films telling the stories of carers of eating disorder sufferers. These films will allow the world to have an insight into what carers, who are so often overlooked, feel and deal with.

Body Gossip also has an education program (Gossip School) which involves educating teenagers in schools and colleges about eating disorders as well as promoting self-esteem, encouraging them to accept their unique bodies and to recognize their worth. As a mother, I cannot extol enough the value of such work. In a world where body-image issues seem inevitable, it is heartening to know that there are campaigns such as these making a difference to the lives of young people. The other half of the donation will allow Gossip School to carry out their important work in underprivileged schools, which would not otherwise have the funds for their program. For more information go to www.bodygossip.org.

CHAPTER 1

WHAT IS AN EATING DISORDER?

Disordered eating, and the mentality which fuels it, make no sense at all. What would possess someone to deny themselves the most basic of human needs – a healthy and balanced diet? If you are a parent, you've become accustomed to providing your child with everything they require – physically and, when you can, emotionally. Finding yourself in a situation where, suddenly, you are unable to fulfil this role is incredibly frustrating. For any carer, the feelings of futility and despair as your loved one destroys their health and happiness with an eating disorder are incredibly difficult to deal with.

Unfortunately, this often goes unacknowledged. In many situations, carers of eating disorder sufferers go through a worse time than the sufferers themselves. Throughout the course of this book you will discover that, as a carer, you are not alone. You will learn that the feelings you are experiencing are normal and natural. Most importantly, you will arm yourself with a real understanding of your loved one's illness and discover the most effective ways to help them towards recovery.

In refusing to eat and exercise in a healthy way, an eating disorder sufferer is running the risk of causing untold harm to their bodies and minds, both temporarily and in the long term. As a carer or concerned friend, we attempt to understand what might trigger someone to starve and deny themselves nutrients, or to binge and purge on a regular basis, or to consume such large quantities of calories that they become clinically obese. Is it nature, or nurture, or both? Can we fairly blame popular culture (magazines, advertising and the media) and the pressures of today's society? Is this a mental illness, a physical condition, or a little of each? We will explore these questions further throughout the book.

Sometimes it can be difficult to determine where 'fussiness' stops and disordered eating begins (and therefore a cause for concern arises). It's difficult to know if someone is genuinely particular about the foods they like and dislike, or whether this desire to control their food intake has wandered into more dangerous territory. Often, anorexics claim suddenly and inexplicably (to those around them) to have embraced vegetarianism, for example. This could be a ploy to further restrict their food intake. It could, equally, however, be a perfectly sincere desire to give up meat and herald a happy, healthy life as a vegetarian.

Bobby Davro, entertainer and father of three daughters between the ages of 10 and 18, has experienced first-hand the precarious balancing act one must play as a parent, always being aware of the issues and monitoring his children's eating habits, but knowing when to intervene and when to take a step back. He says:

It is very important for any parent to be aware of the early signs which can lead to anger issues and, at worst, an eating disorder. Good judgement is both the hardest and most crucial part of your job, as a parent – it's important to avoid escalation of something that could potentially harm not only your child, but the whole family unit.

There is so much information available now; we can end up utterly baffled and vaguely hysterical, and therein lies the problem. Because the term 'eating disorder' covers a multitude of different abuses of food, they can affect people in a multitude of different ways.

Think of the number of people you know who are either on a diet, or constantly declaring their desire to embark upon one. When does this begin to straddle the chasm between (frankly) annoying and actually worrying? Equally, you probably know many people who are slightly overweight. Statistics show that the Western world is rapidly heading toward widespread obesity – but how do you determine the difference between simply enjoying your food and using it as a coping mechanism?

It has been argued that what we would now be quick to brand as 'eating disorders' have in fact been around for centuries, and that our modern obsession and the recent meteoric rise in diagnoses arises less out of a growing trend and more out of our desire to label everything. Of course the same logic could be applied to diabetes and many other illnesses, so this line of reasoning doesn't quite stand up to scrutiny.

When behaviour surrounding food becomes extreme, it is then classed as an eating disorder, but often the patterns of thinking which have infused that behaviour have begun much earlier. The individual habits of a sufferer might not wholly conform to one recognized disorder, but take some traits from each. It can seem like a veritable minefield.

Diagnosis is, therefore, very difficult. Completely healthy but naturally slender people are often accused of being 'anorexic' (it's become something of a pop culture buzzword). Most of the people caught in a binge/purge cycle are a 'normal' BMI or even slightly overweight. The simple lesson is that, however tempting it might be, it is not possible to make a conclusive diagnosis simply from a visual assessment.

We should be on the alert for the signs of an eating disorder when someone displays anxiety in a situation where food will be a) present and b) unavoidable. People become anxious around food for any number of reasons, but this anxiety can grow to the extent that it dominates every waking thought.

This leads us back to our original point: disordered eating goes hand in hand with disordered thinking. This is not just because of the underlying emotional issues which infuse the disorder, but because nutrition affects the delicate balance of chemicals in the brain. Lack of nutrients, therefore, interrupts reasoned thought. That's exactly why your attempts to confront the problem might have seemed so utterly ineffectual. The logic that *you* would apply to the situation is just not accessible to the sufferer.

Eating disorder sufferers cannot be told to 'pull themselves together', to 'stop doing that' or to 'just eat.' Many carers and friends become incredibly angry and frustrated as they perceive an eating disorder as something the sufferer *chooses* to inflict upon themselves, of their own volition. This is just not the case. My daughter Samantha's twin sister, Charlotte, recalls: 'What pulled me through was knowing that Sam was still inside, and it was not her talking and acting at that time, it was the eating disorder.'

The above paints a pretty bleak picture. The good news, however, is that, also contrary to popular belief, full and lasting recovery from an eating disorder *is* possible.

The most common question I am asked by concerned friends and relatives of eating disorder sufferers is simply *What can I do?* The most crucial step is to develop a better understanding of eating disorders – not just the physical symptoms, but the state of mind which infuses them.

Throughout this book we will explore all of the above, without apportioning blame or recriminations. It is all too easy for the people around eating disorder sufferers to blame themselves. This blame is not only often misplaced, it actually delays recovery – it places an obstacle in the way of your loved one's journey back to health. Guilt is a destructive and ultimately pointless emotion, and we will not entertain it here.

There is so little support and understanding available for carers – all carers, whether they be family, friends, colleagues or professionals, need to work together not only to support the sufferer but each other, too. Any chink in your armour can be exploited by an eating disorder, which is why it is crucial that carers must communicate. Marg Oaten, MBE, founder of SEED Eating Disorder Support Services in Hull, one of the UK's leading support groups for all those affected by eating disorders, says: 'As husband and wife we supported each other and always made sure we were united in our approach and clear about what needed to happen in order to get our daughter on the right track to recovery.'

I hope this book will give you the clarity you need in order to provide the consistent and coherent support that is needed by everyone involved.

One of the most dangerous myths surrounding eating disorders is that they are a life sentence. It is distressing to see people managing their conditions, learning to cope with them on a day-by-day basis, with both the sufferer and their carers resigned to the fact that this is as good as it gets.

Hope with Eating Disorders will show you that full and lasting recovery is possible. It will allow you to see how you and your loved one can free yourselves from the prison of eating disorders and enjoy the liberty of a life which isn't dictated by food, once more.

Through communication, positive thinking, love and, most importantly, *hope*, there is a way through the maze of eating disorders and a path back to happiness and health for both the sufferer and their carers.

CHAPTER 2

ANOREXIA, BULIMIA AND OVER-EATING

ANOREXIA NERVOSA

In its simplest form, anorexia nervosa is the severe restriction of food intake, over a period of time. It is impossible to be either more specific or more descriptive than this. While there are other elements which categorize this dangerous illness, each and every sufferer is unique, and each and every one of them experiences the disorder in a different way.

The term 'anorexia' was first coined by Sir William Gull, one of Queen Victoria's personal physicians, back in 1873. (The word *anorexia* is of Greek origin, *an* being the prefix for 'little' and *orexis* for 'appetite', meaning 'a lack of desire to eat'.) This fact in itself answers any accusations that anorexia nervosa is a new phenomenon.

Anorexia is not an illness of the body; it is an illness of the mind. In fact, it has the highest mortality rate of any mental illness. Anorexia cannot be cured by treating the physical symptoms alone; it is the mind which must be treated. Because of this, it terrifies and fascinates people in equal measure.

If you are a carer of someone suffering from anorexia, the people around you probably won't know what to do or say, in order to help. You may feel isolated, because any support network available to you won't come to your aid in the same way they would if your loved one had a physical injury, or even a better understood illness.

Marg Oaten reinforces this point when she says: 'In some ways, we found it a strain to explain it to family members – all cared deeply, but some just didn't get the whole eating disorder illness.'

You may turn to the internet, thinking it might help you to understand a bit more, or you may scour articles in the press on the condition. This could find you ending up even more baffled and frustrated. As there is so much varied information available through various channels it is very difficult to know what applies to you and your own situation. I aim to provide the information that I think really matters, with no agenda other than helping you to understand all the eating disorders and the signs to look for.

A lot of people, teenagers and young women in particular, 'flirt' with anorexia at some point in their lives. In a few cases this will develop into something life-threatening. As a parent or carer, it's important to know where the distinction lies, and what should concern you.

Of all the many eating disorders, anorexia undoubtedly gets the most press. This is both a good thing, because it raises awareness, and potentially dangerous because the information out there can perpetuate myths which in actuality prevent carers from seeing the signs of anorexia early on.

Sadly, anorexia can be the media's friend because, when it becomes very severe, it is visually shocking. There is also a worrying tendency for it to be portrayed as 'glamorous', with sufferers often citing a desire to conform to society's beauty ideal as the reason behind their compulsion to starve themselves. In reality, the causal factors behind their illness are almost certainly manifold and highly complex. There is very rarely one solitary motive for disordered eating. The sufferer's numerous motivations intertwine, fuelling one another and the condition. If we persist in trying to boil anorexia down to one fundamental contributory factor, we will only continue to give rise to a number of myths and misconceptions.

We have all seen the headlines which scream 'I weighed just 4½ stone!' These stories are usually accompanied by a picture of the subject, looking shockingly skeletal, in their underwear. As a result, many people believe that the most important symptom of anorexia is weight loss, and that the lower the sufferer's weight, the more severe their issue. This isn't necessarily true. Again, it is always crucial for you to bear in mind that anorexia is a mental illness, not a physical one.

The trend for 'poorly pictures' (which were advised against in a set of guidelines issued by Beat, the UK's largest eating disorder charity, in 2010), can in reality prevent sufferers from seeking the help they need. We have been led to believe that if someone is a 'normal' weight, they cannot, by definition, have an eating disorder. Again, this isn't always true.

What truly categorizes anorexia is obsession. To reach the astonishingly low weights which are reported in the press, a sufferer would have required time, not to mention a fairly small frame and high metabolic rate to begin with. Some people starve for years without physically reaching a weight which is perceived as an urgent problem by the medical community. Are they still anorexic? The answer is a resounding *yes*.

Using weight to diagnose anorexia is like seeing how far someone can walk before determining if they have a broken leg. It simply doesn't take into account the issues at the source of the disorder.

It also leads us to draw the conclusion that in order to rehabilitate an anorexic, we should force them to eat. Once their weight has reached a 'normal level' they are cured … right? … *wrong*! We must remember that the underlying emotional issue, the mind-based obsession which is at the disorder's origin, is still present. It is very important to remember that this is a mental illness we are dealing with and not just a physical one. This is precisely why so many anorexia sufferers relapse almost immediately after leaving professional care.

So, the first and most crucial hurdle to overcome in diagnosing anorexia is the idea that you must weigh your loved one. In doing so you are searching for symptoms, not causes.

Kimberley developed anorexia after having first been diagnosed with obsessive-compulsive disorder (OCD). Interestingly, OCD and anorexia share a number of common traits and have often been shown to go hand in hand. Gail, Kimberley's mother, shares her thoughts and beliefs when she says: 'I firmly believe that, if you treat the mind, you treat the body. The majority of professionals treat the body first, leaving the mind unrecovered.'

By focusing on physical symptoms only, we're missing the emotional signs. Knowing this is the carer's greatest ally. Obsession is a difficult thing to identify, but it can also be spotted early, before anorexia becomes physically life-threatening.

For example, a father I have worked with said that, looking back, the first sign of his daughter's anorexia was when she began to wear his clothes. At the time, he reasoned that she simply liked wearing them. In retrospect, of course, she was trying to cover her body and, more specifically, conceal her weight loss.

Very few people wake up one morning and simply decide to stop eating, for no reason at all.

As this book progresses, we will explore the experiences of sufferers and carers from all walks of life who have been affected by eating disorders, and in particular their road to recovery. One of these case studies centres around Eva, whose battle with anorexia began in her early teens. She is described by her mother, Kyra, as, 'Never being happy with her body shape. She was teased, causing a loss of confidence in her body, so that her self-esteem plummeted and she developed anorexia.' What Kyra has quite rightly observed, here, is that loss of confidence and self-esteem was a precursor to her daughter's eventual condition.

My own daughter, Samantha, developed anorexia at the same age as Eva. She had contracted a virus which led to her losing a little weight. As a result she received a lot of compliments, which tapped into a pre-existing insecurity she had concerning her body shape. She wanted to continue to lose weight thereafter, but it eventually got out of control. It really was as simple, and as complicated, as that.

I have since learned that the circumstances in which Samantha's eating disorder developed are reasonably common. Post-virus is a dangerous time in terms of the potential for an eating disorder to arise. Of course it is by no means certain that if, for example, your child has had gastric flu, they will then develop anorexia, but the above is something I believe is worth knowing. After all, as a carer, knowledge is your best friend.

If your loved one has a pre-existing insecurity, anorexia, or indeed any eating disorder, can begin very innocently.

Many of the parents I have worked with and have spoken to have been encouraged to think that, because eating disorders are such a serious and dramatic illness, they must have arisen out of a previous traumatic incident. They then blame themselves for not having 'noticed'. In my experience, this is rarely the case. In fact, eating disorders usually arise out of something very innocent. There is always the possibility that the illness originates in something more sinister, but this is by no means a certainty. Again, the stories that are reported on by the media tend to be those which involve abuse, or trauma, because stories like these are considered to be more powerful.

A former anorexic recently appeared on a popular daytime television programme. She was asked during the interview why her eating disorder had begun. 'I just threw my sandwiches away, one day,' she said. The interviewer persisted, 'Yes, but why? Why did you throw your sandwiches away?' She thought for a minute, then replied, 'I just did.' This conversational pattern was repeated at least three times before the interviewer accepted that, as far as this sufferer was concerned, the problem began on the day she threw her sandwiches away.

Some people are by their nature sensitive and prone to insecurity. It takes very little for that sensitivity to be tapped into. There is not a great deal that unites absolutely all eating disorder sufferers, because, as discussed, each patient, and their story, is unique and individual. They do, however, all have one thing in common: low self-esteem.

It is this low self-worth which gives birth to a mind-based issue which, in turn, evolves into an eating disorder. As a carer, looking out for huge quantities of weight-loss is missing a vital opportunity to address the problem at an early stage. Zoe, 21, my daughter Sam's best friend, talks about when she first realized how ill Sam actually was:

At first I wasn't properly aware of what she was going through, no one was. Because we spent so much time together it was easy to ignore the weight loss. When I saw the effect Sam's illness was having on her family, that's when it hit me. It took over their lives; anorexia controls every thought of every moment, but it felt like more than anything Sam wanted to be treated like a 'normal' person.

Arguably, however, we're all a little critical of our bodies in our image-obsessed culture. Teenagers, in particular, will go through a certain degree of worry and angst concerning their physical appearance during the normal course of growing up. So where does the need for concern arise?

Justin, who is 20 and a friend of my daughter's, reflects on his awareness of her eating disorder, during their teens:

I'd noticed that Sam had been losing weight, but this was not uncommon, as many of the girls in my year were hitting puberty and changing physically. I felt quite ashamed that I had not noticed it before, but I suppose that it's not really the sort of thing that a 13-year-old boy looks out for.

For an anorexic, food dominates their every waking thought. They are constantly fantasizing about how to avoid food, and what they will not eat. It is a common misconception that anorexics do not like food. The vast majority love it. They are obsessed with it. They see food as a powerful and irresistible enemy, something to be eschewed at all costs in their physical lives, but which is omnipresent in their thoughts. This is why the idea that anorexics have a lot of 'willpower' and are 'in control' is so very inaccurate. They have relinquished all control over their minds.

In the early stages, signs that should concern you are:

- an encyclopaedic knowledge of the calorific values of foods

- frequently weighing themselves (often more than once per day)

- secretive behaviour in situations where food is unavoidable (putting food in a napkin or feeding it to the dog, for example)

- a wide range of excuses as to why they will not be present at mealtimes ('I ate a big lunch' or 'I am going to have dinner at a friend's house')

- either constantly deflecting attention from, or drawing attention to, any resultant weight loss

- picking fault with their body

- excessive exercising

- spending a lot of time on websites that revolve around food and body image

- prizing weight loss above other life interests (giving up previous hobbies and friends)

- a sudden interest in cooking (but not eating)

This last symptom is perhaps a surprising side-effect for the early stages of anorexia, however it is very common. Sufferers will cook huge meals, bake cakes and puddings for their friends and family, but eat nothing themselves. Perversely, they wish to test themselves, to tempt themselves by touching, handling and smelling food, but not ingesting it. It's also symptomatic of the degree to which anorexics think about food, despite avoiding it. Eva's best friend Chelsea recalls the first time she felt really concerned was when she noticed her friend undertaking this bizarre practice. She says: 'My friend had a small barbeque and invited everyone over. She cooked all this food but never touched any of it and instead had a small salad. That's when I realized it was getting really bad.'

As a carer it's important to be vigilant about this – the fact that anorexics often cook and bake might fool you into believing that they are eating. It is important to take note of what they actually eat.

Indisputably, however, the biggest indication of anorexia is a distinct change in personality. In retrospect, this is usually what carers of anorexics noticed first. At the time the sudden change in behaviour (e.g. being irritable, short tempered, distant or withdrawn) had seemed inexplicable, but it was only when their loved one's illness developed that they recognized it as a sign.

What differentiates anorexia from a diet is the secrecy involved. An anorexic knows, instinctively and from a fairly early stage, that their condition needs to be hidden. They are aware that the people around them, who care for them, will try to stop them restricting their food intake. They will convince themselves that these people are either jealous, or do not understand. Their minds house two seemingly contradictory notions: That avoiding food is the most important thing that they can do, but that it is also somehow wrong and must be hidden from others.

This is just one example of the constant internal dialogue that takes place in the mind of an anorexic. They are always arguing with themselves, and this is exhausting. They will appear tired, and they will seem withdrawn and preoccupied.

As a result, a large proportion of an anorexic's time is spent attempting to cover their tracks. They may become introverted. Losses of confidence, concentration or ability to interact socially are all key signs.

It is absolutely vital always to bear in mind that the anorexic's mind is not a logical place. Siblings and friends of anorexics, in particular, tend to become increasingly exasperated, wondering why they simply won't eat. They sometimes tell them to 'stop it,' rationalizing that their friend or loved one is starving themself to gain attention.

Again, this is because of a lack of understanding of anorexia as an illness. It is often perceived by the people around the sufferer as being a selfish condition. While this is true to an extent, objectively speaking, it is important always to bear in mind that the sufferer cannot help themself. Anorexia is not a lifestyle choice. The sufferer is possessed by their illness. Harbouring resentment and ill-feeling causes the situation to escalate, and arguments will ensue. Mealtimes and social gatherings will be a battleground in any event, without these feelings of bitterness thrown into the mix.

Suzanne Dando, former British Olympic gymnast, reflects back on the effect her anorexia had on her family:

Recovery is a slow process. Methodical? Yes. Fraught with ups and downs? Of course. There were days when it seemed easier to let the disease win and return to abnormal behaviour, secrecy, being insular and moody, and shunning all those who are desperate to help.

It's a disease that makes us selfish. Not until we are firmly on the road to recovery can we appreciate just how much pain we inflict on our parents and loved ones, who have to stand by and watch us try to destroy ourselves both physically and mentally.

While we will see in a later chapter that there have recently been much higher instances of male eating disorders, those men not directly affected often have the most trouble in comprehending an eating disorder. Fathers, brothers and male partners aren't lacking in sympathy or concern, they merely often have difficulty in understanding the warped thinking of the anorexic mind. By trying to tackle anorexia with logic, they become increasingly frustrated, arguments ensue and the sufferer sinks further into themselves.

Charles, father to a recovered anorexic, speaks of the frustration he felt during his daughter Eva's illness:

I watched a rapid change, as my loving, caring, bubbly and vivacious daughter turned into an obsessive, dull-eyed shell. As her father, surely I could solve this problem, as I do daily in everyday life? Successful, powerful, and without limits as to financial resources, I felt positive that I could turn this around quickly. How wrong could I be! I entered a battle which I wasn't prepared for, and started a learning curve that would often leave me devastated and frustrated. Over a two-year period, I watched my little girl lie, cheat, bully, manipulate, plead, cry, threaten and use any method open to her to avoid eating and to satisfy the anorexic noises constantly in her head.

Opportunities to communicate with an anorexic about how they feel can be rare, and should be encouraged. The information you receive from them will prove vital in the recovery process. Don't apply logic; accept that their mind is a confused place and that, in talking, they are providing you with an important glimpse into its inner workings.

David, whose girlfriend of four years suffered from an eating disorder, says that the best piece of advice he could extend to carers is 'not to judge'. He says: 'There were times when my girlfriend was very open with me about her eating disorder. I realized it was important not to act shocked, or create conflict, because then she'd stop communicating with me.'

Which brings us onto another salient fact: the brain requires energy. In many cases, the effect that malnutrition has on the mind is not only more immediate, but much easier to detect, than the physical symptoms. Becoming forgetful or irritable is commonplace in the early stages of anorexia. If a sufferer is known for being highly efficient in their job, then suddenly begins to report that their colleagues are 'picking on them' because they 'forgot something', this usually means they have lost the ability to concentrate. The same applies to a sudden plummeting in school grades.

Starving the brain also leads to a lack of creative ability. Be aware of a sudden unwillingness or inability to undertake creative endeavours which were previously a pleasure, such as art, writing or music.

Forgetting to lock the front door, leaving the iron on, losing their personal possessions – these are all signs of the absent-mindedness which accompanies not feeding the brain. Of course, some people are naturally forgetful so, again, I must emphasize that the most crucial symptom is a drastic change in personality.

In these early stages, and indeed throughout the course of your loved one's illness and recovery, communication is your most powerful tool; this not only benefits the sufferer but the carers as well. Try to spend as much time together doing other things that do not focus on the eating disorder, such as watching a film, going shopping or to the cinema, sharing a less active hobby, etc. By doing this, hopefully all concerned will relax, find it easier to talk and reap the benefits.

Communication can be the best way for you and your loved one to negotiate yourselves out of the maze.

My daughter's friend Justin gives his thoughts on how communication helped to turn things around for us:

> *Sam started to become more and more withdrawn, spending more time in her room than she had done before. It was quite strange as this withdrawal seemed to gradually lead to the whole family spending less time with each other. It*

was frustrating for me at the time, as I could just see that they needed to talk to each other. Once they had realized this, looking back that's the point that they started to make progress. It was great when they started talking and spending more time with each other again.

Gentle encouragement on the subject of food, support, lack of judgement and positivity are all strategies you can use to prevent the condition from worsening.

Of course, these subtle emotional signs are easy to miss, or to mistake for the more common-or-garden teenage angst or mild depression. If anorexia has developed to a stage where the physical symptoms become more prominent, you will notice:

- erratic, sparse or non-existent periods in girls and women

- fine downy hair growing on the body (and in particular on the back)

- hair loss/thinning of hair on the head

- the sufferer often complains they feel cold, even in warm temperatures, and their nose, fingertips and toes are cold to the touch

- the sufferer becomes pale and looks drawn

- bad posture – either because they don't have the energy to hold themselves upright, or because they want to apologize for their bodies

- fainting/dizzy spells

- frequent episodes of crying or tearfulness

- anger/mood swings

- wearing baggy clothes or layering to hide the weight loss

The biggest tell-tale sign is, however, in my experience, the appearance of the eyes. The difference between someone who is naturally very slender and someone who has starved themselves into that state can be ascertained simply by looking them in the eye. The anorexic's eyes are sunken and vacant. Their eyes look 'haunted', because the sufferer is literally haunted by their condition. Their mind is consumed by their disorder and so they have retreated into themselves. Their energy is used up in introspection, and they have nothing left to give the outside world.

If your loved one exhibits the physical symptoms of anorexia, do not plough your time and energy into blaming yourself, or berating yourself for allowing things to reach this stage. Instead, take the opportunity to learn about the illness itself and the various treatments available to you when they do reach out to you for help. We will explore these later on.

It's also important to separate fact from fiction and to attempt to understand fully what is happening in the mind of your loved one.

Sarah wrote the following, which highlights the contradictions in her thinking when she suffered from anorexia:

At my lowest weight during my anorexia, looking in the mirror became an obsession. Many people have a misconception of what anorexics see; when I looked in the mirror I didn't see a fat person in front of me, it wasn't the image that kept me from not eating. I knew I was thin. Just wasn't thin enough. It also wasn't about how I was perceived by other people. I didn't care if I had a typically good body. I wanted a thin body. It isn't what anorexics see in the mirror which makes them continue to starve themselves, it's the feeling that anorexia gives them. It's the same as giving a drug addict drugs or giving alcoholics a drink. It takes a certain type of person to develop anorexia – they have to be slightly depressed and insecure. When people feel like something is missing inside them, they try to fill it with something. To me, not eating filled that hole; it made me feel I had something, which is why it is so hard to beat as you cling on to the feeling of losing weight.

Sarah has identified here the single biggest and most all-pervading myth which surrounds anorexia – namely that anorexics see a large person when they look in the mirror. They know they are thin, they simply do not think they are thin enough – and they will never be thin enough while they continue in this mind-set.

An anorexic might pick out a single perceived 'flaw' and focus on it (for example their thighs, bottom or stomach). Because of their unrelenting belief that this 'problem area' is disproportionate or ugly, they are then less aware of how slender the other areas of their body have become. They don't always do this, but this, I believe, is where the idea that anorexics see a 'fat person' in the mirror has arisen from.

Many carers reason that they are counteracting their loved one's condition by encouraging them to see how truly thin they have become. This is counterproductive, firstly because an anorexic usually knows how thin they are, and secondly because they are perversely proud of it and thrive on any mention of it.

Anorexics see weight-loss as an achievement, their sole life-goal. Drawing attention to it is the equivalent of patting them on the back and saying 'well done!' Tamsin, a recovered anorexic, demonstrates this when she remembers:

I was in a queue at school, waiting to use the pay-phone to call my mum (these were the days before mobiles). A girl who was in my class turned around to face me, with a look of absolute disgust, and said, 'Tamsin eat something, put some weight on, you look revoltingly skinny.' I spent the rest of the day floating on air, so proud of myself that I really must, at last, be thin. I resolved to eat even less from then on.

It is important to emphasize at this stage that my motive for dispelling the common myths surrounding anorexia is not to paint a bleak picture, or to suggest that the condition is a life sentence, or beyond treatment. Sadly, there is no quick fix; it takes time, patience and understanding. But please remember that anorexia is curable. The example of my own daughter, as well as of the others described in this book and countless more, proves this. But the disease needs to be correctly understood.

As a carer, the most important things to acknowledge are
that each anorexia patient will experience the illness in a way
which is unique to them, and that you must therefore approach
treatment in the way which is correct for them. There is no cure-
all solution, but that does not mean that there is no solution
at all. Later, I will describe in depth all the various treatments
available for eating disorders. One of these, or a combination
of them, can help your loved one towards recovery. In the
meantime, knowledge is crucial and communication is key.

Another thing which is important to bear in mind when the
recovery process begins, is that any step forward, however
small objectively, will seem momentous in the mind of an
anorexic. Often, anorexics believe they are 'doing really well'
because they are eating enough to sustain their weight, when
your ultimate aim, of course, is for them to put on weight.
You'll feel frustrated with them at this point, and wish that
they would try harder. Be patient. Bear in mind they have
gone from actively wanting to become thinner and thinner to
eating enough so that they do not lose any more weight, and
acknowledge that this is a positive step in the right direction.
After all, everyone likes to be praised, and a person suffering
from an eating disorder is no different. If anything, I have found
that positive compliments and praise can help to combat the
negative feelings and thoughts in the sufferer's mind, fuelling
them to try harder, as they are often keen to please those
around them. This then helps to break the negative cycle
shared between the sufferer and carers, and can lead to a more
positive environment for all concerned.

Bear in mind also, however, that simply because they are eating enough to sustain their body, that does not mean that they are consuming sufficient calories to heal their mind. Feeding the brain is what silences the internal urgings of anorexia and allows the sufferer to let go of their illness. The body prioritizes the vital internal organs over the mind, so this may take some time. Emotional progress usually follows physical progress. Food intake can stabilize the sufferer, but to recover, they must want to get better. It takes time, patience and unconditional love to exorcise these demons.

My daughter Samantha reinforces this point when she says:

> *The key to my recovery was my mum and finding my own willpower within me to make myself get better. Mum made me realize that there was more to life than my illness, and helped me come to terms with the fact that I had a problem and must get better or be ill and waste my life.*

Below is a summary of the familiar 'facts' which are often quoted in relation to anorexia. They are, as we have discovered, myths which prevent us from really understanding the illness.

MYTH: If an anorexic gains weight, they are recovering.

TRUTH: Anorexia (and, indeed, any other eating disorder) is a mental illness, like depression. While there are physical symptoms, it is the mind-based issues which need to be addressed. Remember: if you treat the mind, the mind will treat the body.

MYTH: Anorexia is ultimately about 'control'.

TRUTH: A lot of sufferers refer to 'control' because that is how their condition appears to them. However, from an outside perspective, they have lost control totally.

MYTH: Anorexics have always experienced a significant and traumatic incident.

TRUTH: Some anorexia arises in response to trauma, some does not. This varies from patient to patient. A significant or dramatic past incident is by no means a certainty.

MYTH: Anorexics see a 'fat' person when they look in the mirror.

TRUTH: Often, anorexics are aware of how thin they have become, they simply do not consider it to be thin enough. (This myth arises from the fact that, often, anorexics pick and focus on one perceived 'flaw', such as their stomach or thighs, and obsess upon it, rather than seeing their body as a whole.)

MYTH: Anorexics always try to conceal their weight loss.

TRUTH: Some anorexics will wear baggy clothes in a bid to hide their weight loss. Others will try to draw attention to their slimmer frame. Again, this varies from patient to patient.

MYTH: Anorexics only eat lettuce leaves.

TRUTH: An anorexic will restrict their food intake. However, they might allow themselves a very small amount of chocolate each day. The food stuff they choose is irrelevant; it is the restriction which is important.

MYTH: Anorexia only affects teenage girls.

TRUTH: As we will discover throughout the course of this book, anorexia and other eating disorders affect both genders and all age ranges, races and social backgrounds.

MYTH: Anorexics are classic over-achievers and/or perfectionists.

TRUTH: Just as anorexics come from all walks of life, they also have a variety of different personalities.

Summary
When people think 'eating disorder', they usually automatically think of anorexia. However, there are dozens of different ways to have a dysfunctional relationship with food and your body, many of which remain totally unacknowledged.

BULIMIA NERVOSA

Bulimia nervosa is more common than anorexia, but tends to attract less attention and press. It is also often said in the same breath – 'anorexia and bulimia' – as if the two conditions are interchangeable, which is not the case.

Bulimia is a dangerous illness and, although steps are being taken to raise awareness, sadly, just like anorexia, there is a general lack of understanding.

Bulimia nervosa is distinguished by the act of bingeing and purging. Sufferers first gorge on a huge amount of food (either objectively speaking, or what they consider to be a huge portion), and this is followed by what are known as 'compensatory behaviours'. These 'behaviours' most commonly involve the sufferer forcing themselves to vomit, taking laxatives, or a combination of the two. This is often coupled with periods of starvation, excessive exercising or even sleeping for large quantities of time to 'work off' the calories consumed. Lori Henry, a former dancer turned writer, describes in her book detailing her battle with bulimia, how she would exercise for hours to counteract her binges:

> *After a binge, I would try to make myself throw up to rid my body of the disgusting feeling of fullness, but it only made me feel better for a minute. So I began going directly to the treadmill at home and running for two hours until I was shaky and pale.*

Just as with anorexia, there are many different ways to be bulimic. Like anorexia, bulimia is a mental illness. Also like anorexia, it is woefully misunderstood.

Bulimia is arguably the hardest of all eating disorders to identify and diagnose, because the physical symptoms are the least obvious to the people around the sufferer. The good news for carers is that bulimia also has a very high success rate for permanent recovery (responding particularly well to neuro-linguistic programming (NLP) and hypnosis, both of which will be discussed in more detail in Chapter 5).

If anorexia is difficult to understand from an outside perspective, bulimia might be even harder. Contrary to popular belief, bulimia does not always result in huge amounts of weight loss. This is what makes the illness so baffling, but it also demonstrates perfectly that eating disorders are not solely related to body image. We can see, through bulimic behaviour, how a disordered attitude towards food arises out of a truly disordered mind.

A mother of a recovered sufferer shares her thoughts: 'We need to be particularly vigilant in order to recognize bulimia, which, contrary to popular belief, causes little or no weight loss but instead destroys both the physical and mental wellbeing.'

Bulimia has many sub-types and, like all eating disorders, it affects each individual sufferer in a unique way. The classic definition of bulimia involves patients bingeing on huge quantities of food. Because it is physically impossible to purge the body of everything eaten during a binge, sufferers are often a 'normal' weight or even slightly overweight.

Bulimics are likely to lose weight initially, and then gradually gain it, regaining or even exceeding their starting weight. They can also fluctuate wildly in weight during their illness.

However, it is important to note that the lack of obvious external physical symptoms does not detract from the severity of the illness. The physical appearance of most bulimia sufferers does not reflect the damage they are doing to themselves internally, and this is one of the disorder's most dangerous factors.

It also means that the sufferer may find that the people around them are less sympathetic towards their situation than if they were anorexic. People are, by their very nature, more likely to understand and sympathize with an illness whose damage they can see. You may find that, as a carer, you are isolated. Your loved one probably appears physically healthy, but, as we will see later, is likely to behave strangely, becoming moody, withdrawn or prone to emotional outbursts.

There is also a stigma attached to bulimia, as there is with all mental illnesses – the illness is intrinsically linked with feelings of shame and disgust, both for the sufferers themselves and for their carers. This combination of factors isolates the outside world.

People misguidedly believe that the solution to anorexia is forcing the sufferer to eat. Although this, as we have seen in the previous section, is not the case, it is at least something they believe they can proactively do. With bulimia, there is no such solution. Bulimia is distasteful to most people. It involves overindulgence and bodily fluids. It isn't a pleasant illness to contemplate. Most choose to stay away entirely, because they cannot understand – it is easier for people to sweep the issue to one side rather than confront it.

Sophia, whose 30-year-old daughter has now recovered after struggling with bulimia for almost a decade, says:

We were at a party recently and someone remarked on how lovely my daughter was looking 'these days'. I replied 'Yes, that is because she is well these days.*' I just let it hang in the air between us. I thought to myself, 'Where was your concern when she was suffering?'*

Like alcoholism and drug abuse, people don't discuss bulimia openly. It is whispered about behind closed doors. People fear what they cannot understand. And, to an extent, who can blame them? The compulsion to stuff oneself to bursting with huge quantities of food and then to force it out of the body by various means is utterly unfathomable, to most.

A great deal of this misunderstanding arises out of the idea that it is the binge that the sufferer 'enjoys', and the purge which they feel they must undertake because they do not want to gain weight. This is overly simplistic. As bulimia progresses, the sufferer might binge on foods they don't even like – or on frozen or out-of-date foods, just to give them the opportunity to purge. It is the act of purging – the physical release, the punishment of the body and mind – which the bulimic craves.

Sometimes the media can contribute to some of the misunderstanding surrounding the illness. Owing to their tendency to focus on the visual, case studies where the sufferer has experienced a dramatic amount of weight loss are usually picked and presented to the public. In reality, the subjects of these case studies are likely to be suffering from less common sub-types of 'traditional' bulimia, which involve actively restricting their portion sizes yet still feeling the desire to 'purge'. Because there is an element of anorexic thought patterns and behaviours associated with these sub-types of bulimia, the sufferer often believes that they are 'bingeing' and yet, in practice, they are eating relatively small amounts of food.

Sandra, a former bulimic, worked in an eating disorder clinic for two years. She emphasizes this point when she says:

We had two sets of 'workbooks' for patients to take away with them when they left, one for anorexics and one for bulimics. We tailored them to each patient, and printed them off before their session, ready for when they left. Halfway through this one girl's session, the therapist burst into my room and told me to print off material for bulimics. 'She isn't anorexic!' he said 'she just told me she binges!' As a former bulimic, I could tell just from looking at this girl that the problem was anorexia, not bulimia. I told him to ask her what she was 'bingeing' on. It turned out to be two digestive biscuits. That is not bulimia.

It is important to distinguish bulimic behaviour from bulimia nervosa. For a bulimic, the desire to binge and purge consumes their every waking thought. Social meals become a military-style operation: they scope out the venue to see where the toilets are, and how they will plan their escape from the table. Like anorexics, these social occasions are rare because both types of sufferer actually fear food, but for totally different reasons. Bulimics see food as a best friend and a mortal enemy. They look forward to being alone with it, but they hate it and themselves for what that will inevitably entail.

The idea that anorexia and bulimia are interchangeable is a myth. While it is fairly common for anorexics to practise some bulimic behaviour in addition to starving themselves, and for bulimics to starve for periods of time as a form of purging, they are two very distinct illnesses.

Originally, the word 'bulimia' derives from the Greek *boulimia*, meaning 'appetite of an ox'. It is more closely linked with compulsive eating, addiction and even self-harm than with anorexia, as we will see below.

To identify bulimia in the early stages, the crucial signs to look out for revolve around evidence of the binge/purge cycle. These include:

- suddenly becoming more reclusive, rejecting invitations to social occasions and eschewing company

- if the sufferer still lives at home, large quantities of food disappearing mysteriously

- a 'secret stash' of foods somewhere in the sufferer's home

- eating very quickly, without seeming to enjoy the food

- inexplicable and sudden lack of money (because it has been spent on food)

- finding an excuse to go to the bathroom directly after meals (for instance, 'to have a bath')

- dehydration

- constant cold or flu-like symptoms – runny nose, streaming eyes, sore throat

The last of these will be the most prominent, in these early stages. The act of forcing oneself to vomit causes mucus to build up and streaming of the eyes and nose. The sufferer will also invariably wake up with a sore throat and blocked nose.

The biggest hurdle to overcome on a bulimic's road to recovery is conquering the feelings of shame and guilt which give rise to the urgent need for secrecy which categorizes the illness. By nature, the public are less sympathetic to disorders which involve eating huge quantities of food, as opposed to constantly denying it.

Richard, the partner of a severe bulimic, emphasizes below the helplessness he felt, attempting to support his girlfriend through an illness the effects of which no one could see:

> *Without a doubt, the hardest thing about being the boyfriend of someone with an eating disorder is that it's not your secret to tell. I never betrayed her trust by telling my friends and family. I ended up cancelling so many family get-togethers and nights out with friends, because she would have an emotional 'episode' or her eating disorder would flare up, just before, and that meant I couldn't go. In the end, I stopped accepting invitations. Of course, because they didn't know what was going on, my friends and family thought she was the girlfriend from hell, who was deliberately keeping me away from them.*

Often bulimics have great difficulty in confronting their issue and in speaking openly about it to their friends and family because they believe they will be labelled as 'greedy', or as having no self-control. Unlike anorexia, there is absolutely no misguided notion that bulimia might be 'glamorous' in the public perception.

Whereas anorexics often feel proud of their abilities to starve, and wear their weight loss like a badge of honour, bulimics are plagued with constant feelings of shame and self-disgust. They fear judgement and criticism, and this fear can permeate all areas of their lives, so that eventually they over-react to even the smallest criticism of their work, personality or appearance in their professional and private lives.

The way to handle bulimia, therefore, is with sympathy and without judgement. Bulimics require, above all else, an acknowledgement of what they are going through. They need to feel that the people around them are at least willing to understand. They do not need to be told to 'stop doing that,' or that they are stupid or greedy.

As time goes on, the bulimic lives with the knowledge that, in all probability, everyone around them knows, and even this makes them feel like a failure. They usually see themselves as a failed anorexic, too lacking in willpower to starve. They often become paranoid, imagining that everyone is laughing at them. As a carer, it is your job to dispel these feelings and provide unconditional support.

It's also important to note that a large part of bulimia can be habit. Often sufferers aren't exactly sure how or why their condition started, but they find themselves unable to stop, despite wanting to. A huge key in treating bulimia is breaking habits and associations. For example, a bulimic might always binge and purge in the evening when they come home from work. They do not want to, but they have become so practised in doing it they find themselves unable to stop, much like a smoker. Studies show it takes as little as a few weeks for a habit to develop. The good news is, it takes a similarly short time to break those habits – however, the underlying emotional factors and low self-esteem must also be addressed.

It is important, at this stage, to note that communication with bulimics doesn't always yield the reaction you want or expect. Both physically and emotionally, the bulimic is in turmoil. They might lash out, or say things they don't mean, blame you for interfering or tell you they do not need you. They don't mean this. Carers need the strength to continue plugging away at the channels of communication and to distinguish between when it is the sufferer and when it is their illness talking. Carers of all eating disorder sufferers require a thick skin. It's difficult not to take personal comments, or anger, to heart. But it is also an essential part of the person you love's recovery.

As stated above, one of the most all-pervading myths persisting about bulimia in the world today is that it is weight loss which motivates the disorder. As with all eating disorders, the somewhat warped reasoning behind it is complex and many-faceted. Bulimics often express a desire to lose weight, or lack of confidence in their appearance, yet their disorder is more likely to be a coping mechanism for dealing with difficult emotions.

Ivett, who has recovered from bulimia, says:

> *After having bulimia for ten years, I realized it wasn't making me slim! I was eating a lot and getting bigger. The problem was that when I started to eat I couldn't stop. I spent so much money on food – literally money down the toilet! So I decided one day to stop doing it. I now have breakfast, lunch and dinner. I never miss them. I have lost weight! I am so much happier now – and cannot believe that I ever made myself sick!*

You will often hear a bulimic say 'If only I could lose two stone, my life would be so much better.' The important part of that sentence is not that they wish to lose two stone, it is that they feel their lives could be better.

Emily, a former bulimic, says:

> *My father drummed it into me from a young age that I was overweight and unpleasant to look at. At around the age of 20 I heard about bulimia through a radio programme and thought it sounded like a good way to control my weight.*

Emily battled bulimia for the next 25 years. It would have been easy for her to reconcile herself to her fate. However, brilliantly, she has now been in recovery for three years. The crucial change happened when she realized she needed help. She says:

> *It got to the point where I was really fed up with myself and my behaviour, leading to a strong desire to want to change. It was a gradual process, for me, which occurred over time, like a layering effect, enabling me to grow stronger and stronger.*

Until one day I realized I had detached myself from my old behaviours and had moved on, leaving them behind me in my past.

Bulimia shares characteristics with self-harm, the binge-and-purge cycle providing a release for emotional tension and a way to inflict punishment on the body for feelings of guilt or inadequacy. Again, as with anorexia, it is not certain that significant trauma has occurred in the sufferer's past. The contingent factor is the patient's sensitivity and innate inability to cope with difficult situations, rather than the severity of their life circumstances.

Lack of body confidence is a symptom, not a cause: general insecurity often manifests itself as a preoccupation with appearance (which in turn tends to be misinterpreted as vanity or superficiality), but it is not this which is at the heart of the matter. A bulimic's demeanour can seem wildly overconfident, in contrast to the anorexic's, which is invariably characterized by a desire to disappear. Bulimics can swing between seeming desperate for attention and being consumed by self-hatred. It is the inconsistency in their behaviour and emotions which is the salient factor.

A bulimic's thought and behaviour patterns mirror the extremes of their eating habits. The first and most important sign that someone might be suffering from bulimia is, without doubt, mood swings. These will become more and more severe as the sufferer's condition worsens. Richard, whose partner was bulimic, says:

The scariest thing was the effect my girlfriend's eating disorder had on her mind. Looking back, there were a lot of times when she didn't treat me particularly well, and I was always left questioning whether it was her, or her eating disorder, that made her behave that way.

Bulimics are moody for a number of reasons. Firstly, because being sick on a regular basis, even for a short amount of time, usually results in deficiencies in both iron and potassium, and the imbalances this causes in the body and brain result in erratic behaviour. Secondly, because the sufferer's thoughts are constantly invaded by unpleasant emotions, and these often make themselves evident in the patient's language and interaction with others. Thirdly, because the extent to which the desire to binge and purge takes over the sufferer's life leads, in most cases, to depression.

Depression and eating disorders are part and parcel of one another, and this is never more true than of the bulimic. The binge-and-purge process is a physical expression of inner turmoil. It is a cry for help, aimed at the self. The longer someone has suffered from bulimia, the more fragile and volatile their mental state will be. Bulimics tend to lose a lot of friends. They will experience:

- feelings of depression or anxiety

- mood swings

- irritability

- tearfulness

- expressions of wild elation, or anger, for no apparent reason

- inability to concentrate

- frequently feeling sleepy

In addition, the imbalance in their nutrition, while not necessarily resulting in weight loss, can lead to the following:

- thinning of hair/hair loss

- bad circulation

- weak nails

- dry/flaky skin

- weakening of the immune system: being prone to picking up colds, flu, etc.

The act of making themselves sick over a prolonged period of time will also cause puffiness around the jaw line (as the glands become swollen) and erosion of the teeth. The sufferer may also have red or raw knuckles if they are using their fingers to force themselves to vomit.

As we have seen, there are many myths and misconceptions surrounding bulimia – it is a deeply misunderstood condition. Below is a summary of the most common myths, and the facts:

MYTH: Bulimics are underweight.

TRUTH: Bulimics are often slightly overweight, or what is considered a 'normal' weight. It is even less possible to diagnose bulimia by weighing the patient than it is for anorexia.

MYTH: Bulimia and anorexia are interchangeable.

TRUTH: Bulimia and anorexia are two distinct illnesses. While they may borrow specific behaviours from one another, they manifest themselves in totally different ways, physically and psychologically.

MYTH: Bulimia is ultimately about losing weight.

TRUTH: Bulimics might be labouring under the false idea that their condition will lead to weight loss, but this is also accompanied by feelings of inadequacy, guilt, shame and self-loathing. It is these emotions which ultimately fuel the disease.

MYTH: Bulimia is less dangerous than anorexia.

TRUTH: While anorexia statistically has a higher mortality rate than bulimia, bulimia can be deadly (most often bulimia-related deaths are caused by a heart attack, resulting from the strain vomiting places on the heart). There are also a myriad of serious physical and psychological symptoms, as listed above.

MYTH: Bulimia is about vanity.

TRUTH: Bulimia is akin to self-harm. It develops as a coping mechanism for difficult emotions and is fuelled by low self-esteem. While a bulimic might act confident, it is simply that: an act.

MYTH: There is a certain type of person who is more likely to suffer from bulimia.

TRUTH: Bulimia affects people of all ages, races, walks of life and of both genders.

Summary

Bulimia can be conquered. There is a wide range of highly effective treatments available. As Ivett and Emily's testimonials show, the most important thing is that the sufferer must *want* to get better. Bulimics invariably reach a stage where they are physically and emotionally tired of their illness. They don't know why they are doing it anymore. They want to stop, but they might believe that they are unable to. This is the prime time for them to receive treatment. Over the chapters that follow, you will learn that it is possible for them to go on to lead happy and healthy lives.

OVER-EATING: BINGE EATING AND COMPULSIVE EATING

If bulimia is not given the correct amount of sympathy, then the plight of the over-eater is even worse. We are constantly being told about the Western world's 'obesity epidemic', and overweight people are often victimized and perceived as villains. Over-eating is an eating disorder, and there are many things that can be done to combat it.

If carers of anorexics and bulimics feel isolated, the issue is even worse for carers of over-eaters. Public opinion never seems to take into account that the reasons behind over-eating could be more complex than pure and simple greed. Just like anorexia and bulimia, over-eating can be a mental illness.

Like all other eating disorders, over-eating usually has its roots in emotions and is the result of low self-esteem. (The 'epidemic' in the Western world is, in fact, one of low self-esteem!) People find different ways to deal with this – some eat less, some eat more, equally, some drink to excess, take drugs or smoke – these are all issues which need to be addressed with more than a simple 'stop doing that.'

Craig, 20, has this to say about over-eating during his teenage years:

> *Eating and food itself were my only source of pleasure, which seemed to fill a huge void in my life at the time. Food had become an addiction – something I knew was having a negative impact on my confidence and self-esteem, but I felt I couldn't change it.*

When eating disorders are discussed, over-eating is often overlooked. It isn't seen as being in the same 'league' as anorexia or bulimia.

This might be because a large proportion of the UK and US population are overweight, and don't perceive themselves as having an eating disorder. And many of them don't. So we ask again, where is the line between enjoying your food and using it as an emotional crutch?

The answer lies in the notion of 'mindful eating'. Over-eating becomes a problem when the sufferer isn't aware of what they consume. Over-eaters tend not to chew, and to eat while engaging in other everyday activities (such as watching television, social networking on their computers, texting or speaking on the telephone, or working at their desks). Many tend to 'graze' constantly, eating sweets and other bite-sized snacks consistently throughout the day.

Over-eaters are also likely to be in genuine denial about how much they eat. Sufferers will say 'I don't eat all day' because they instantly forget what they have, in reality, consumed.

The reasons behind over-eating must also be examined. Over-eaters often 'reward' themselves after a hard day at work or school, or a personal triumph, with high-calorie foods. They'll also turn to the same foods in times of emotional crisis or upset.

Over-eaters will tell you they feel 'hungry', but it is an emotional hunger as opposed to a physical one. The two have become confused in the sufferer's mind. Cravings for food in response to uncomfortable emotions, like boredom or loneliness, feel so powerful it is difficult to distinguish them from genuine hunger.

Melanie, 24, describes how over-eating can arise out of feelings of boredom and inadequacy:

I turned to eating after the breakdown of my parents' marriage. I had a full year of not doing a lot, and sat around at home with just my part-time job to keep me busy, and spent hours on end with food as my only comfort. It gave me something to do. I was bored and down about everything and I felt that crisps and sweets would make me feel better. They didn't at all. But when there is nothing, and your family and friends are busy, food is always there. I look back now, as I am really trying hard to lose the weight I gained, wishing I had found comfort in something else. But at the time, it was all I felt I really had.

A lot of this has its roots in social convention. When we are young we become so accustomed to being rewarded with food – going out to dinner to celebrate good grades, having a special cake on our birthday, or being consoled with 'treats' when things go badly – that we carry this habit into our adult lives. Couple this with the trend for fast food and constant food-based advertising and we can see how food can become addictive.

It's a popular theory among psychologists that over-eating has its roots in childhood, for the very reasons listed above. However, while being 'treated' to and comforted by food in childhood is pretty much universal, not everyone ultimately becomes an over-eater. Again, the contingent factors are the sufferer's sensitivity and self-esteem.

Food often masks the real problems in an over-eater's life. They believe their life would be better if they could conquer their over-eating and lose weight, but this is, in actuality, a red herring. Over-eaters are often dissatisfied or frustrated with their love lives, careers or other life circumstances. They eat as a means of coping with this and, as they gain weight, they sink further into their unhappiness. So the situation becomes a vicious circle.

Over-eaters are also often so keen not to repeat the food mistakes of the previous day, they will go through short periods of starvation. This is, of course, counterproductive, because starvation causes the body to binge when food is reintroduced.

It's also worth noting that the over-eater may be dehydrated. Often, thirst is mistaken for hunger. Very few of us drink enough water, and over-eaters, with their tendency not to look after their more general health, are no exception.

Signs that differentiate over-eating as an issue are:

- eating in response to an upsetting event

- low self-esteem

- general life dissatisfaction

- eating quickly, without chewing

- eating 'mindlessly', while engaging in other activities

- using their weight as an excuse for putting off taking steps to improve their lives

As a carer, again, your most effective weapons will be compassion, understanding and communication. Never make the sufferer feel 'greedy'. Do not restrict their food intake. Do not make them feel that eating is 'wrong'. This only leads to secretive behaviour and, perversely, the desire to eat even more. Instead, let them know that they are entitled to eat, while at the same time exploring the underlying emotions which are fuelling their over-eating.

It should be noted that there is a difference between restricting food intake and actively 'enabling' the sufferer's over-eating. It is a fine line that can be difficult to tread successfully.

Do not make the sufferer feel as though over-eating, or being large, are part of their identity. Do not describe them as 'always being big' or 'loving their food'. Doing so subtly but powerfully builds food into the sufferer's identity. Allow them to explore who they are outside food. Encourage them to think about what they are good at and what they want from their lives. You will often find that, when they feel happier and more fulfilled, the over-eating stops of its own accord.

One again, communication is absolutely vital – but it is not your job as a carer to draw attention to the sufferer's eating habits. They will already know they are over-eating, and they will already be riddled with guilt and shame because of this. The role of a carer is to help the sufferer explore the reasons behind their condition, to find out what holes in their emotional, professional and private lives they are attempting to fill with food.

Over-eating is often referred to as 'binge eating' or 'compulsive over-eating'. These differ slightly. Let's take a closer look at each of these disorders.

Binge Eating Disorder
Binge eating is, as you would expect, very closely linked to bulimia (the difference being that the sufferer will not purge

after they have binged). The two disorders also share the unfortunate similarity of being shrouded in secrecy. Just as bulimics often wish they had the 'willpower' to be anorexic, it is not uncommon to hear a binge eater express a desire to be 'better' at purging.

Binge eaters often have a hidden stash of food, stockpiled by numerous visits to different supermarkets so as not to arouse suspicion. Binge eating does not take place in response to physical hunger. In fact, the binge eater might not be able to recognize the signs of physical hunger, because they are so used to eating in response to their emotions.

Because society teaches us to be ashamed of our urge to eat, and because of the huge and unusual quantities they consume, binge eating disorder sufferers often feel a constant sense of embarrassment, driving them to even greater lengths to conceal their behaviour. Often perceived as anti-social, their tendency to hide themselves away results from the dual factors of a) of never wanting to be too far from food, and b) not wishing to put themselves in a situation where a friend or loved one might uncover their terrible secret.

Alternatively, the sufferer may adopt a 'larger than life' persona, again in an attempt to hide their condition and persuade the people they encounter (and perhaps even themselves) that they are happy with their size. Jennifer's story, below, demonstrates this:

I'd been friends with Sally for years and always thought of her as the 'jolly' overweight girl, who was perfectly at ease with her size. She was always giggling, flirting and showing off her oversized curves in short skirts. Gradually, as I spent more time with her, however, I noticed the mood swings. If she had a bit too much to drink, one minute she'd be the life and soul of the party, the next she would be sitting in the corner, sulking or sometimes crying and no one could ever work out what had caused the switch. Once, someone asked her if she was upset because she was bigger than the other women in the bar. She denied it, but responded by becoming incredibly angry, so we could see a nerve had been touched. We later discovered that she was eating a full large takeaway pizza, a tub of ice cream and drinking a bottle of wine every single night in her flat, alone. She was desperate to stop but didn't know how. I don't see her much anymore. Her mood swings isolated her from most of her mates. But I believe that her eating habits were at the root of them.

Bingeing can escalate rapidly, or it can be a habit which develops gradually over a number of years. Other than weight gain, as the story above demonstrates it can be difficult for the sufferer's friends and family to pinpoint the problem, or to know what action to take when they do. There are also 'occasional binge eaters' – the constant yearning to eat is present but the sufferer will set limits on themselves, yo-yoing between what they consider to be acceptable 'limits'. Physically there may be no symptoms at all for an occasional binge eater, but psychologically there are still issues which need to be addressed.

Having said that, 'emotional hunger' (which we touched on above) is something all of us will have experienced. Part of the issue is the attachment of a moral judgement in our perception of food (advertising has a lot to answer for in this regard) – it's somehow considered 'naughty' to eat chocolate, so we persuade ourselves that we 'deserve' it for whatever reason. Every time you've bought yourself a high-calorie but delicious snack on your way home from work because you've had a 'hard day', you've had a glimpse into the mentality of a binge eater.

Sufferers of course *can* get better. Recovery essentially hinges on breaking the associations the sufferer has made between positive emotions and certain foods. Binge eating is an addiction and, just like alcoholism or drug addiction, recovery depends upon conquering cravings. Unlike drug users and drinkers, however, it's not possible for a binge eater to go 'cold turkey' and give up the source of their addiction entirely. Instead, food must be consigned to a much more minor role in the sufferer's life – they must learn to eat to live, and stop living to eat.

Compulsive Over-eating

Compulsive over-eating is, in its simplest form, 'food addiction'. As the name suggests, it's almost identical in every way to binge eating disorder.

The most obvious difference is that a compulsive over-eater will graze in between binges. A compulsive over-eater is incapable of passing their fridge or cupboards without retrieving a snack.

The feel-good chemicals released by high-calorie foods have become so addictive that the sufferer seeks a further 'hit' each time the feeling begins to fade (they are similar to smokers in this regard).

A compulsive over-eater embarks upon a love affair with food. Being unable to tear oneself away from a subject and fantasizing about it constantly, to the extent that it disrupts concentration, are usually emotions we associate with the first flushes of romantic endearment. Food marketers can exploit this (we all have a tendency towards it to some degree), ensuring our perception of food and sexuality are inextricably linked.

In exactly the same way that sexual desire often elicits shame, the compulsive over-eater will feel incredibly guilty for their state of mind. There is no lack of awareness, merely a belief that they are predisposed to be this way and incapable of changing. This is, of course, untrue. They simply require the right combination of guidance and support.

Compulsive and binge eating disorder can lead to:

- **Type 2 diabetes**

- **weak or painful joints**

- **excessive sweating**

- **inability to exercise**

- **shortness of breath**

- heart attacks or other organ failures

- chapped or sore thighs (if the sufferer has thighs that rub together as they walk)

However, these issues are by no means inevitable. Both types of over-eating have been shown to respond well to therapy, in particular to hypnosis. More than any other eating disorder, over-eating can be seen as a life sentence when it is in fact no such thing. While anorexics and bulimics believe it will take a lifetime to conquer their emotional demons completely, over-eaters take on the identity and persona of an overweight person and believe that they must live with it. Because being overweight affects the choices they make and the activities they engage in, it does, to an extent, shape their personality.

However, the key lies in allowing the sufferer to recognize that over-eating is not who they are. Full recovery and a life free from over-eating are attainable with the right mind-set, help and support.

Mikyla Dodd, an actress most famous for her role in *Hollyoaks* and her later appearance in *Celebrity Fit Club*, has battled with compulsive eating and is passionate about changing attitudes and approaches to it. She sums up the most common misconception surrounding over-eating and how she believes it should be tackled:

The biology of the situation is simple but the cause is far more complex and requires a much more in-depth approach to achieve lasting success and to like/value yourself more than you do food.

*I think we should be able to discuss [eating disorders]
openly as an issue instead of being so afraid to address
it in case we cause further damage. To ignore it actually
exacerbates the feelings of loneliness and isolation that then,
in turn, create a bigger problem.*

SUMMARY – THE TEN MOST IMPORTANT TIPS FOR CARERS OF EATING DISORDER SUFFERERS

1. Do everything you can to open channels of communication between you and the sufferer. You do not have to directly discuss their eating or exercise habits in order to do this. Simply by spending quality time with the sufferer, discussing their favourite television programme or hobbies can sometimes be enough to make them feel comfortable and to encourage them to speak openly with you.

2. Listen to what the sufferer is saying. However illogical it may seem, you are being given a valuable insight into their mind-set.

3. Do not judge and try not to be shocked by anything they tell you.

4. Be prepared for the sufferer to act out of character and say things they do not mean. Remember that it is their illness talking, not them.

5. Remember that you are playing a waiting game. Sufferers cannot get better until they really want to. However, they can be sustained in the meantime, and this is part of your role.

6. Do not blame yourself.

7. Don't look for reasons that don't exist – remember that a lot of eating disorders start quite innocently.

8. Look after yourself – remember that you need to be well in order to help your loved one.

9. Knowledge is your greatest weapon – use this frustrating time to research which treatments might work and to really understand the mind-set of your loved one.

10. Talk to other carers – find support groups or online forums to help you feel less isolated during this difficult time.

Caring for someone with an eating disorder can push everyone involved to their limits and beyond, however I would like to reiterate that, with the right support, understanding, unconditional love, patience and time, *all* eating disorders can be beaten and full recovery is possible.

CHAPTER 3

OTHER EATING DISORDERS

EDNOS

This is an acronym for 'eating disorder not otherwise specified'.

Technically, more people suffer from EDNOS than anorexia and bulimia put together. Like anorexia or bulimia, EDNOS manifests itself differently in each sufferer, but because it is characterized by symptoms from a variety of different eating disorders, there's even more scope for an EDNOS to make itself evident in a range of different ways.

No two people have the same relationship with food, and there are literally hundreds of ways to have an unhealthy dynamic with your diet. The purpose of this chapter is to help you identify some of the destructive behaviours which have been recognized and classed as EDNOS. This will aid you in distinguishing the boundary between merely unusual food and exercise behaviours, and dangerous ones.

Before doing so, it is worth noting that there are two distinct diagnoses of EDNOS, which can lead to confusion. If someone principally displays all the symptoms of anorexia, for example, but occasionally binges and purges, this would be classified as EDNOS. Many eating disorder sufferers go through phases, first starving for periods of time and then, because they are so very hungry, bingeing and purging out of a sense of guilt.

It is not uncommon for sufferers to consider themselves to have both anorexia and bulimia for this reason. In medical terms, this would be classed as EDNOS. However, it's very uncommon to have anorexia and bulimia simultaneously and, under closer scrutiny, the sufferer is likely to be suffering from either one or the other.

Adam, who realized he was anorexic after being diagnosed with EDNOS, says:

> *Sometimes I'd be so hungry, I'd give into the temptation to eat. After days of starvation I'd hold out for as long as I could before caving in. Afterwards I'd feel I'd let myself down, and I'd make myself sick and double my workout in the gym. Looking back, this wasn't anorexia/bulimia or EDNOS. I'd just used an element of bulimia to assist me in being anorexic. Understanding this helped my path to recovery.*

The other use of the word EDNOS, and the one we will be focusing on in this chapter, is used to describe disordered eating which falls outside the definition of anorexia, bulimia or over-eating.

There are various practices and rituals which people develop surrounding food which are both physically and psychologically unhealthy. They are also unsociable, dominate the sufferer's life and prevent them from enjoying themselves or fulfilling their potential. During the course of this chapter, we will help you to be able to identify these disorders.

Of course it would be impossible to describe every single way to have disordered thinking with regards to food and exercise. However, the following are the most common types of EDNOS.

Extreme Dieting

With an estimated 43 per cent of people in the Western world presently 'on a diet', it is little wonder that occasionally this can become both dangerous and extreme.

When dieting becomes an obsession, it's usually characterized by strict rules which the sufferer believes they cannot deviate from under any circumstances.

Maria, who spent most of her twenties and thirties yo-yo dieting, remembers her mentality at the time:

You become more and strict with yourself. You push yourself to see how little you can survive on, or how 'healthy' you can be. And by healthy I mean no fat, no dairy, no carbs, which of course isn't healthy at all. In the end it becomes an obsession. And you become so fixated on your diet, it stops you living your life. You can't go out for a meal; you can't enjoy chocolate in front of the telly with your boyfriend. Your simple pleasures are taken away.

As Maria's testimony demonstrates, extreme dieters set themselves up to fail because the rules they impose are so unrealistic. They constantly batter their self-esteem because they have not succeeded in living up to their own strict guidelines.

You'll also often find the extreme dieter attaching a moral significance to certain foods. Some foods are 'good' and others 'bad'. This inevitably leads to the subject fantasizing constantly about 'forbidden' foods. In situations where their resolve is weakened and they eat these 'forbidden' foods, for example a social occasion or when they have been drinking alcohol, the dieter may feel compelled to purge.

This is distinct from bulimia because the sufferer does not binge in the same way and their binge/purge behaviour is sporadic and inconsistent. However, the condition is very dangerous psychologically, not least because the sufferer is fixated on food.

Routine Starvation

Sufferers of this condition see periods of starvation as 'necessary' in order to maintain their physique. They will often go without food for a few days at a time. They do not consider this to be unhealthy, or worrying, but simply a way of life.

Elise, a model, says:

In my industry it's considered totally acceptable to starve yourself totally, surviving only on black coffee and gum, for two days before a shoot or show. This was considered to be a necessary part of the job, and because I ate relatively normally the rest of the time, I had no idea I could be doing any long-term damage to my body.

Because routine starvation often does not result in the more extreme physical symptoms of anorexia, such as loss of periods, sufferers would not be diagnosed as anorexic. However, they are likely to be malnourished and have hormonal imbalances as a result of their behaviour. They also run the risk of long-term health problems such as osteoporosis.

Purging without Bingeing

This condition is categorized by eating small portions of food and then purging, by the sufferer either making themselves sick or taking laxatives.

Because sufferers do not binge on large quantities of food, they miss an essential element in the diagnosis of bulimia. The condition shares more in common with anorexia, or orthorexia, which is defined below.

Diet Pill Addiction

The internet has made it incredibly simple to purchase illegal, banned or prescription-only substances which promote slimming. These drugs are seen as being a 'quick fix', with some claiming to increase metabolism and others that they purge the body of all fat within any food consumed.

Because these pills often contain, or emulate, recreational drugs such as speed, they provide a chemical 'high' in addition to causing weight loss. They are highly addictive, and sufferers of this condition will find that they need to take increasingly large quantities of the drug in order to achieve the same 'buzz'.

The suppliers of these drugs, in order to entice people into what is usually a lengthy period of taking these drugs, often offer a 'free month-long trial', knowing that this will, in most cases, result in the person wanting or needing more. It is a psychological as opposed to a physical dependence, however it feels very real and powerful to the diet pill addict.

Lauren, who took an illegal diet pill in increasingly high doses for almost two years, recalls how she fell into this dangerous trap:

> A friend told me about a website where you could buy pills that not only made you skinny but also so you never felt like eating. I started taking two every day. They made me feel super switched-on. I never felt hungry but I also never felt tired. I was losing weight so fast – I thought it was the magic solution to all my problems. I started taking more and more. It was only when I experienced heart palpitations and passed out in college one day that I was scared into stopping.

Diet pill addiction has all the same perils as addiction to any other illegal substance.

Chewing and Spitting

This practice arises out of the misguided belief that if one chews food and then spits it out, one does not consume the calories within that foodstuff. Of course, this isn't true. Just like bulimia, the body retains some of the food which is ultimately ejected.

Compulsive Night Eating

This disorder is usually caused by sufferers starving throughout the day. They long to have what they perceive as the 'willpower' to starve constantly.

Their bodies will cry out for food by the time evening arrives, resulting in powerful physical craving, causing them to eat in secret throughout the night. This disorder is characterized by feelings of shame and of guilt. It is shrouded in secrecy.

Lucy, a client of mine, has had first-hand experience of this, having eaten during the night for three years:

> *I would starve all day and go to sleep pleased with my efforts. When I woke up in the middle of the night, sometimes it was almost as though I was sleep-walking. I would go downstairs and straight to the fridge, unaware of what I was eating. Sometimes I would even wake up halfway through eating a peanut butter sandwich, with no recollection of preparing it. The next morning I would be aware that I had eaten the night before and say to myself, 'I won't do that again' and starve myself all day to compensate. So of course it was a vicious circle. I broke the habit when I realized I needed to eat during the day to stop my body crying out for food at night.*

Sufferers often claim to be 'on a diet' but the people around them notice that they do not eat their specially procured 'diet foods'. These remain untouched.

As well as playing havoc with the metabolism, this disorder results in extreme tiredness and mood swings.

Compulsive Exercise

Gym memberships are practically mandatory in today's society. With our increasingly sedentary lifestyles, gyms are seen as providing the solution – allowing us to undertake some much-needed exercise.

Problems can arise when the need to exercise becomes a compulsion and the sufferer becomes obsessive.

Sufferers of compulsive exercise will work out for longer than advised, and sometimes continue to exercise through injuries. The constant physical strain placed on the body means that sufferers are always hungry, and they often feel guilty for this. They may starve and binge in cycles.

Fitness expert and health writer Nicki Waterman says:

> *Excessive exercise offers a built-in reinforcement. It increases endorphin levels, providing the individual with a sense of wellbeing. The endorphin levels remain high, even though the individual is seriously, and perhaps permanently, compromising their own health. Studies are currently being conducted to ascertain and better understand the addictive nature of exercise.*
>
> *Extreme or compulsive exercise is dangerous. The most significant dangers of extreme exercise are overuse syndromes such as stress fractures, low heart rate, amenorrhea and osteoporosis.*

Nicki offers the following advice:

In trying to evaluate whether exercise levels have gone from reasonable to excessive, the following questions can be asked:

- Does the person feel guilty if they miss their workout?

- Do they still exercise when they are sick or hurt?

- Would they miss going out with friends or spending time with family to ensure they achieved their workout?

- Do they freak out if they miss a workout?

- Do they calculate how much to exercise, based on how much they eat?

- Do they have trouble sitting still, because they are not burning calories?

- If they are unable to exercise, do they visibly cut back on what they eat?

These are all symptomatic of a mind-based obsession with exercise.

EDNOS – Summary

In many ways, our culture of extremes can be blamed for EDNOS. We are encouraged to diet and to exercise, while being constantly bombarded with advertisements for food.

Many people, particularly in younger generations, have lost the ability to cook completely, opting instead for convenience and fast foods laden with chemicals. We are given a lot of information about 'nutrition', under many guises. Some of this information is genuine, some utterly bogus. Food is seen as the enemy, not something which nourishes and sustains us, but something which must be avoided or minimized at all costs, or indulged in amid feelings of guilt and secrecy.

Many of us have sedentary lifestyles, sitting in front of a PC for much of the day and watching television for recreation. We, rightly, feel the need to compensate for this, and many do this in a healthy and balanced way – taking care of what they eat and exercising moderately. For some, however, the confusion they feel because of the mixed messages we are fed, as well as the desperate desire to attain a super-slender or very 'buff' beauty aesthetic, can mean their food and exercise habits rage out of control.

When food and exercise dominate someone's life, affecting them detrimentally physically and mentally, this is EDNOS.

OTHER, LESS COMMON DISORDERS – DEFINITIONS

Wannarexia

'Wannarexia' was a term coined to make the distinction between the causal elements of anorexia. Increasingly over recent years, teenagers in particular cite 'fitting in' or wanting to emulate celebrities and models as their reasons for hugely restricting their food intake. Many medical professionals and eating disorder sufferers would argue that this does not fit the criteria for anorexia, which is an intensely private psychological illness, often linked to OCD and feelings of control.

This is a controversial arena, since most experts in the field generally conclude that anorexia arises from a combination of emotional reasons and body dissatisfaction, or at least that the illness is fuelled to some degree by super-slender beauty paradigms. The distinction between anorexia and wannarexia is, therefore, not always crystal clear.

What is certain, however, is that wannarexia is no less dangerous or deadly than anorexia – the symptoms are identical. The difference lies in the sufferer's reasons for starving themselves.

Orthorexia

This term was coined as recently as 1997. The sufferer becomes obsessed with healthy eating to the extent that it totally dominates their lives, in the same way that occurs with the fixations of the anorexic or bulimic.

Orthorexics will scrutinize deeply any food they consume and how it is prepared. In extreme cases, the orthorexic will refuse to eat food which they have not prepared themselves, in order to ensure it conforms to the strict rules they have set themselves. The sufferer will convince themselves that additives are 'poisonous'. They have a tendency to criticize the eating habits of their friends and family, lecturing them on all aspects of food and interrogating them on how exactly theirs was prepared. They will have an encyclopaedic knowledge of calories, vitamins and nutrients, but will feel that they alone are an authority on how this information should be interpreted.

Orthorexia is born out of a noble intention to eat healthily, which is then magnified and taken to extremes (fuelled in no small way by a media industry which can be incredibly condemnatory in this regard). Like an anorexic, the orthorexic's obsessive thinking and behaviour will render them virtually incapable of maintaining normal relationships or managing any other aspect of their everyday lives. The severely restrictive nature of their diet will often, ironically, leave them nutrient deficient, which will further impair their ability to think logically.

The condition can develop into anorexia, although initially weight loss is not the orthorexic's intention.

Bigorexia

This is also known as 'muscle dysmorphia'. It differs from compulsive exercise in that the focus is entirely on muscle building.

Bigorexia is often described as 'anorexia in reverse' (to the outside observer it can certainly appear that way). Whereas an anorexic will never be thin enough, a bigorexic can never be as muscular as they desire. Bigorexia affects hundreds of thousands of men (and some women, too) throughout the world. Some will miss important events and work so that they can schedule in an extra workout; others will continue to train through severe pain and even broken bones.

As you might expect, bigorexia is mainly prevalent among weight-lifters, although increasingly it is affecting people in other professions as well. It frequently goes hand in hand with drug abuse, as sufferers are tempted to use anabolic steroids to further build muscle.

While the causes of bigorexia are not known, many have concluded that the increasing pressure on men to conform to a 'buff' physical aesthetic, combined with the increasingly normalized expectation of gym attendance, are to blame.

Fatorexia

This is a pop culture term which describes someone who is overweight but unable or unwilling to acknowledge it. It is believed that fatorexics see a slim figure when they look in the mirror.

Drunkorexia

This slang term originated in colleges and universities. It mostly affects the 18–24 age group and is characterized by starving all day to 'conserve' calories which can then be 'used' in a drinking binge in the evening. As one ex-sufferer observed, 'It's like the Weight Watchers points system gone totally mental.'

The perceived advantage, other than avoidance of weight gain, is that drinking on an empty stomach leads to faster inebriation, hence saving money. Consequences include liver damage, malnutrition and osteoporosis.

Manorexia

This is a slang term for anorexia in men and boys. As discussed earlier, anorexia increasingly affects men and is not an exclusive term, so campaigners for male eating disorder awareness often take offence to this term being used.

Pica Disorder

Pica is Latin for 'magpie', reputedly a bird that will eat anything.

Sufferers of pica disorder eat non-food substances in addition to their normal diet. It is possible to ingest soil, chalk, paint, plaster, glue, insects, leaves, gravel, clay, hair, soap, laundry detergent, flour and raw potatoes. The sufferer will often have a craving for a specific one of these substances.

While the issue may remain hidden, consequences include damage to the intestines, parasitic infection, poisoning or dental injury. Treatment for any nutritional deficiency arising from pica disorder may also need treatment for the psychological element.

Pica tends to be found mainly in children up to the age of two years and pregnant women. Women who experience bizarre cravings during pregnancy often find the compulsion to eat these unsuitable substances so strong it is impossible to ignore, but will keep their eating habits secret because they are embarrassed.

Research suggests that pica is caused by vitamin deficiency and yet, bafflingly, the substance craved often does not contain the vitamin the sufferer is deficient in!

Geophagy

Geophagy mirrors the traits of pica disorder, differing only in that the sufferer eats soil and earthy substances alone.

SUMMARY

This brief guide to terms will hopefully help you to gain a familiarity with conditions which you might see described in the press or online under the topic of eating disorders. Some are recognized medical definitions, others are simply slang terms for sociological phenomena. All the disorders defined have been diagnosed relatively recently.

GLOSSARY

CHAPTER FOUR

SEEKING TREATMENT

The bridge between sickness and treatment in eating disorder patients is a precarious one to navigate, not only for the patient themselves, but for the people surrounding them. Often the temptation is for parents and carers to blame themselves, which unfortunately sometimes can be exacerbated by those responsible for carrying out the treatment. A good therapist knows that the causal reasons for eating disorders are quite often simple and seemingly insignificant. A throwaway comment or the type of teasing most children encounter at some stage in their school years can spark the beginnings of an eating disorder in one person, whereas it would have no effect whatsoever on another. It is all contingent upon a number of factors.

Sometimes, of course, eating disorders do arise from trauma, abuse and violence in the home or outside it. However, because these are the dramatic stories that are inevitably chosen to be reported upon, we are led to believe that these can be the only causes. When someone exhibits the symptoms of an eating disorder, the people around them often assume a traumatic incident has occurred of which they are unaware, and wrongly blame themselves for not having noticed or prevented it.

There is also an overwhelming tendency to blame parents. Possibly because the medical profession want, by nature, to diagnose, to find solutions and reasons, to prescribe cures and to tie the entire illness up neatly and succinctly, they often fail to comprehend the complexity and subtlety of eating disorders. Marg Oaten experienced terrible prejudice in this regard: 'I, in particular, was treated appallingly, and made to feel inadequate as a mum and the cause of the entire eating disorder.'

After diagnosis, many parents or partners of eating disorder sufferers make *themselves* ill by worrying, by blaming themselves, by raking over the past with a fine-toothed comb and by frantically trying to pinpoint where they went wrong. Sleepless nights, high levels of stress and even depression ensue. This is totally counterproductive, because the feelings of guilt run two ways – eating disorder sufferers tend to have a hugely overdeveloped sense of guilt, which will be magnified when they see the effect their illness has had on their loved ones. Their solution to these feelings of shame is usually to bury themselves further in their illness, and so the situation becomes a vicious circle.

It's also important for parents, carers and concerned friends to be well enough to be complicit in the process of recovery. It is essential for all concerned that carers try to maintain their own physical and emotional wellbeing during this incredibly difficult time. Whether the sufferer is young and still living at home, or older, the people around them will be of the utmost importance in supporting and guiding them towards health and recovery. Not isolating yourself, and maintaining good relationships with friends can also help to maintain your emotional equilibrium, as a carer. My own close friend, Kate, says:

During this stressful time, the only way I felt able to help Lynn was to be there for her when she needed to talk, or have a shoulder to cry on. I hadn't had any previous experience of anorexia, so I didn't feel equipped to offer advice. Hopefully, being available to talk, or just listen, at any time of day or night was some comfort.

(It was!)

In terms of the starting point towards recovery, often someone we know can be in very obvious need of treatment for a body or food issue. The most frustrating thing, however, is when it's obvious to everyone but the person actually suffering.

Eating disorders hinge crucially on denial and self-delusion. In many cases, the conscious and unconscious parts of the sufferer's mind are at war. While they are aware, logically, that what they are subjecting their bodies to is damaging, they also believe overwhelmingly that they are in control and that they are a unique case.

Daphne, 31, says:

In the midst of my bulimia nervosa, I honestly felt no connection at all to other bulimics. My eating disorder was my best friend and my worst enemy rolled into one constant companion. I knew I was doing untold damage to my body, but I honestly thought I was beyond help and that no one could ever really understand. When my friends and family attempted to intervene I was angry and irrational, because I wasn't ready to get better.

Daphne went on to make a complete recovery and has been healthy for four years. Her story highlights the first and most important step towards eating disorder recovery: The sufferer must want to get better. As soul-destroying as it is, attempts to rehabilitate sufferers who aren't yet ready to acknowledge and deal with the problem are likely to prove fruitless. (However, with the assistance of the right kind of therapy and environment, a sufferer can be stabilized, so that their condition does not worsen. Getting actively better is what requires the sufferer to engage totally with treatment.)

For many parents, carers and friends, the reality of this is that they must play a waiting game. There are few things more exasperating than watching someone we care about suffer and being unable to intervene. So what can be done in the meantime?

Again, in this instance, knowledge is power. There are a huge variety of treatments available and it's important to understand what they entail and how they work. In this way, when the sufferer expresses a desire to get better, their friends and family can leap into action and find the most appropriate source of help as quickly as possible. To help you with this, there is a guide to available treatments in the next chapter.

The speed with which you, as a parent or carer, might act at this point in time is also of paramount importance. Often the sufferer might yearn for recovery in peaks and troughs, so it's important to place them in a positive and suitable environment while they're in the correct frame of mind and before any seeds of self-doubt sown by their eating disorder can begin to fester and grow. Providing consistent support throughout the recovery process will mean so much to your loved one. As Gemma Oaten, an actress now aged 27 and Marg Oaten's formerly anorexic daughter, says:

I think I got better because, as well as me taking control, my parents did, too. They didn't just sit back and hand me over to all those units and hospitals. Sometimes they had no choice, especially in the early stages when we were all completely ignorant of what was going on and my life was in the balance. However, my parents pushed the boundaries and fought for the right help for me, whilst educating themselves and really understanding the illness. They also at all times remembered that I was their daughter ... a real person ... I wouldn't be here without them.

As discussed earlier in this book, each eating disorder manifests itself in a unique way, because each sufferer is unique. In the same way, there is no 'ultimate' treatment. While, for example, one anorexia patient might respond incredibly well to a certain treatment, it may have little or no effect on someone else who has also been diagnosed with anorexia. For some, a combination of therapies might be the answer. Whatever the decision, it is essential that the sufferer and their supporters choose a course of therapy which fuels and strengthens their desire to recover, as opposed to drowning and, eventually, killing it.

GENERAL PRACTITIONERS

Unfortunately, seeing a GP for the problem, the most natural and automatic course of action for most people, can be something of a lottery. While some GPs are incredibly knowledgeable and capable in the field of eating disorders (and mental illness more generally), with an average of just six minutes to see each patient, the temptation is often to throw anti-depressants at any mind-based problem.

Of course, our expectations of GPs are often incredibly, and unfairly, high. A general practitioner is, by definition, not expected to be an expert in any particular field. Relying on your GP to have a personal interest in, or extensive knowledge of, eating disorders is therefore something of a gamble.

While awareness of eating disorders and body image is growing, there appears still to be a dearth of practical medical advice available. Elisabeth, whose daughter suffered from anorexia, says: 'On the GP's surgery walls there is information on virtually every other ailment, but nothing about eating disorders. It's almost as if it's the silent time-bomb that no one wants to set off.'

Some of the interviews in this chapter show an alarming lack of facilities and understanding within both the NHS and private healthcare systems for mental health care. GPs are frequently therefore left in a precarious situation, unsure of where to refer patients for specialist help. Adult facilities are also, unfortunately, more sporadic than those designed for under-18s.

There can be little doubt that there is a need for further investment, research and revisions within the health service. Anorexia has the highest death rate of any mental illness, while obesity with all its related health risks is often cited as the single biggest strain on the NHS, so eating disorders are in all respects a pressing problem.

Sophia, the mother of a recovered anorexic son, shares her thoughts and frustrations:

> *We naturally turn to the NHS for help. My experience was one of utter frustration with the lack of adequate resources and knowledge to understand that an eating disorder is a psychological disease.*
>
> *So in the impersonal starkness of a sound-proofed consultation room, out come the dreaded weight charts, BMI tables and diet sheets, I am told that my presence is not necessary …*
>
> *After an anxious hour waiting outside, I am called in to hear they conclude it's OK after all –your teenager does not qualify for further specialist treatment because an optimum 'anorexic' weight/BMI has not been reached (at which point, incidentally, you would find them unable to move, requiring hospitalization and drip-feeding to avoid death). Should we just wait for that, then? Surely prevention is better than cure?*

From the perspective of a GP with a specialist interest in eating disorders, their frustration is invariably that they simply do not have the time to assess their patents objectively. A genuine understanding of any eating disorder involves gaining the patient's trust, encouraging them to be candid, listening to what they have to say and reading between the lines where necessary. All of these processes require time. In an industry dictated by guidelines and targets and under constant scrutiny, time is the one thing most GPs are unable to offer.

Usually, when a sufferer is under the age of 18, parents visit their GP first to voice their concerns. In some instances, they can be made to feel overprotective or unnecessarily dramatic. In particularly archaic medical practices, eating disorders are dismissed as a 'phase' or considered trivial in comparison to other illnesses. This attitude can serve to exacerbate the problem. Emma, who suffered from bulimia, says:

> *When I first approached my GP at university I said, 'I'm making myself sick and I am worried.' Those were my exact words. He weighed me and said, 'Well, you're not underweight.' The way he said it made me feel stupid for even going. I thought about all those girls you see in their underwear in magazines, so skeletal they're painful to look at. And I thought to myself 'They are the ones with the real eating disorders.' I felt like I had no right to ask for help and that I didn't really have a problem.*

It took Emma another six years to seek an alternative treatment. She is now recovered.

The General Practitioners Survey

With such disparity in the expertise, attitudes and compassion shown by General Practitioners, it can be difficult to make an informed decision about whether to approach your doctor initially or to opt instead for private treatment. In an attempt to get a general overview, the following research represents a random cross-section of more than 100 GPs, who kindly agreed to complete a survey for me.

1. What is the most common eating disorder you have treated?

    - Anorexia: 40 per cent

    - Bulimia: 50 per cent

    - EDNOS: 10 per cent

    NB: 100 per cent of GPs surveyed said that they see more overweight or obese patients than those with any other type of food-related problem.

2. Do you think that the media has contributed to the increase in percentage of people suffering from eating disorders?

    - Yes: 70 per cent

    - No: 20 per cent

    - Maybe: 10 per cent

3. Is there a set treatment regime you recommend for eating disorders, or are patients assessed according to their individual needs?

- 100 per cent of GPs surveyed agreed that each case should be assessed independently, according to the needs of the patient and the severity of their illness.

4. What do you believe is the most effective approach to treatment?

- Psychological support: 80 per cent (this includes counselling, cognitive behavioural therapy (CBT), family therapy, referral to specialist eating disorder units and the local mental health unit)

- Physical support: 20 per cent (nutritional therapy, regular blood tests, anti-depressants)

NB: For overweight patients, 100 per cent of GPs recommended diet and exercise programmes. A gastric band operation was recommended for severe cases.

5. Do you think that it is possible to recover from an eating disorder?

- Yes: 90 per cent

- No: 10 per cent

However, among the 90 per cent of doctors who answered in the affirmative, a proviso was made that there is always the possibility of relapse during times of stress. This suggests that the GPs do not in fact tend to believe that *complete* recovery is possible. The same 90 per cent also pointed out that having been in recovery previously armed the sufferer with the knowledge and insight to recover more quickly in the event of relapse.

The general consensus was that there is hope in terms of effectively combating the eating disorder epidemic. Although this runs counter to many of the individual experiences of sufferers, it is important to note that often GPs are rendered ineffectual by a lack of time and specific training, rather than a wilful misunderstanding, and this survey demonstrates that perfectly.

Every sufferer's path to recovery is different, as are their individual experiences of the NHS, private healthcare and any alternative medical professionals they encounter. If one treatment proves ineffective, it absolutely does not mean that the patient is 'incurable'. To emphasize this point, below are a selection of case studies, documenting a journey to health. These stories have been told from the perspective of both the sufferers and their carers, to give a real insight into what this period in time entails and the emotional experience of everyone involved.

THE CRILLY FAMILY

In 2004, my beautiful daughter Samantha was diagnosed with anorexia. Interestingly, Sam is a twin. Her sister Charlotte has never suffered from an eating disorder. This led me to the obvious conclusion that perhaps it isn't reasonable to blame parents for issues surrounding food and body image. In fact, eventually I was drawn to deduce that I, her mother, might just be able to help.

As I watched my family fall apart around me, I came to the realization that I couldn't put our fate in the hands of the external therapists and medical professionals who were so clearly failing to help my daughter. I had to take action – I had to try to treat her myself. It's a common belief that mothers are 'too close' to the problem to influence their child in a positive way during eating disorder treatment. I hope that Sam's story convinces you that this isn't always the case.

Sam was only 13 years of age when I first visited my GP, John Dalzell, to voice my concerns. She was continuing to lose weight at an alarming rate after recovering from a virus (it's not uncommon for anorexia to begin this way). We discussed my fears and he was incredibly supportive.

Sam, who is now fully recovered, also recalls the positive reaction we had from our GP. She says 'My doctor quickly realized my potential problem and the severity of it and gave me his support in every way possible.' He also took the time to understand the dynamics of our family, allowing Charlotte and my husband, Kevin, to be included in these primitive but essential stages of Sam's recovery. Kevin says, 'I turned to our GP for a miracle cure. Of course, there isn't one, but I did get compassion and understanding.'

However, despite our good fortune in having a GP who fully comprehended the issues at stake and reacted appropriately, his hands were still tied by the inner mechanisms of the NHS. There was a 14-week wait for an appointment with the Community Mental Health Team (CMHT). The alternative was a private clinic – an alternative we leapt upon unreservedly, desperate for Sam to show improvement (which sadly she did not). We also remained on the waiting list for NHS treatment.

Sam was referred to an NHS dietician. Charlotte remembers the dietician as being 'very intimidating and extremely unhelpful'. Her treatment was 'cold' and textbook – she seemed reluctant to make the effort to understand Sam as an individual, or the psychology behind her illness. Sam remarked that she 'focused on me gaining weight quickly by using unhealthy high-fat, high-calorie foods, rather than concentrating on my thoughts and feelings towards food.'

The experience made us question the value of nutritional therapy for anorexia, at the time. As Charlotte points out, 'The eating disorder is stronger than the person's own mind' – so how much value can there be in knowing the nutritional value of foods? Equally, we worried about Sam using any knowledge she did gather to lose even more weight. However, I now believe there can be a value in nutritional therapy if the therapist has an adequate knowledge of the mentality which underlies eating disorders and, as Kevin pointed out, 'It would help if everyone had a wider knowledge of healthy eating.'

Devastatingly, not only did the other NHS treatments we tried follow suit, but so did the private treatments. During this time, Sam underwent hypnotherapy, NHS counselling and private counselling, among other numerous and varied treatments which were recommended to us by 'experts' in the field. Sam says, 'None of the treatments in either the private or NHS hospitals were adapted to my individual needs and I felt very much like a number, with no opinion or say in anything.' She also recalls feeling 'at times, degraded.'

None of the less conventional techniques, which have been proven to be very effective in combating eating disorders, were ever offered to Sam as part of either the NHS or private systems. NLP, CBT, thought field therapy (TFT) and Bodytalk were never discussed with us, or even presented as an alternative route when Sam showed no signs of improvement.

It became evident to me that none of the professionals who saw Sam genuinely understood her illness. This was when I took the difficult decision to treat her myself. In retrospect, my technique relied heavily on NLP, a form of therapy which challenges negative patterns of thought and replaces them with positive and affirming ones. At the time I did not recognize that I was using NLP, but having studied the technique since, I now realize that this is where the techniques I was using had their basis. Ultimately, however, what Sam needed, and, I believe, all eating disorder patients require, is unconditional love, time, lots of patience as well as constant support and communication. Communication is especially key, not only between therapist and patient, but between carers and families as well.

In the time when I was working to rehabilitate Sam, she remained in what was a relatively 'normal' life. She still attended school and I had regular meetings with her teachers to discuss her progress and to ensure we were all working harmoniously towards Sam's recovery. The school was also careful to watch over Charlotte during this time and to do whatever they could to limit the emotional effect of her sister's illness. I didn't think it advisable for Sam to lie on our couch all day, thinking of new and innovative ways to starve herself – I felt it was important that she remained in her routine as much as possible, and was therefore able to see what life might be like after recovery.

Sam is, of course, better placed than anyone to describe the effect working with me towards recovery had on her: 'Mum worked *with* me to gradually build up an intake of food I felt comfortable with, so I was then able to feel at ease in social situations, which was so important in building my self-confidence and self-esteem.' Charlotte adds, 'Mum inspired Sammie to see life without her eating disorder and gave her the strength to move on, working slowly and consistently'. Kevin puts it the most succinctly: 'My wife simply loved Sam better' – by which he means I helped her get better through love.

Sam has now been recovered for four years.

Of course there is no 'ultimate treatment' for eating disorders, and different techniques will be more or less effective on different patients. However, therein lies the critical point. As I continue to practise as an eating disorder therapist, it is paramount that each of my clients is treated as an individual, and their therapy is tailored to their specific needs. I learned this from my daughter's experiences, and the principle remains true with every client I have worked with since.

THE MATHERS FAMILY

As my family's story demonstrates, eating disorders have a profound effect on everyone around the sufferer, like a ripple in a pool of water – the consequences are often subtle but far-reaching and significant. The Mathers family story will be told from the perspective of four of its members: Eva, who, like Sam, began her battle with anorexia when she was 13 years old, her mother, Kyra, her father, Charles, and her brother Josh, who is two years older than Eva.

Eva had begun to intensely dislike her body shape from a very early age. At school, a few flippant comments were made referring to Eva's body shape. These comments were not intended with any more malice than the usual playground teasing, but they escalated in Eva's mind, causing her body confidence to plummet further. The cumulative effect was that Eva developed anorexia in her early teens.

Unfortunately for Eva, she did not fare as well as Sam in the GP lottery, and when her parents realized beyond doubt that Eva had a problem and took her to her doctor, she was met with coldness and hostility. It's Kyra's belief that her GP had no awareness of eating disorders as a mental health issue. She says: 'When I realized Eva had a serious issue with her weight we went straight to the GP. He was most unhelpful, saying it was probably a "fad" and that Eva would become bored if we just ignored it!'

Josh recalls the advice they were given at this time, which was, unbelievably, that they should ask Eva, 'Don't you think you should be eating a little more?' at family mealtimes.

Charles's recollection of these events is terrifying. He simply says, 'I firmly believe that if we had followed the first GP's advice Eva would have died.'

Eva describes being 'shipped off to join the other anorexics' in a private residential clinic. The family unanimously agree that placing sufferers with other people enduring the same condition can be incredibly detrimental. Josh says, 'Because she'd been put in a box with other like-minded patients, I felt like they fed off each other, swapping ideas and tips.'

Eva's condition deteriorated. Eva reflects chillingly that she wishes now that her GP 'would have listened to me when I was more in control of my mind and before the horrible twisted voices took over completely.'

Crucially for Eva's recovery, her family recognized that there is more than one path to improved health, and sought alternative options, including two dieticians and private therapists. They chose not to pursue further NHS treatment.

Eva had a mixed experience with dieticians. The first she saw did little to aid her progress, however she then saw a different nutritional expert who was 'more knowledgeable and helpful.'

Charles adds, 'I think seeing the dietician was beneficial for us, but I'm not sure if a wider knowledge of healthy eating helps much.' (It is interesting to note how his perspective differs from that of my husband, Kevin – further evidence for my belief that no two sufferers and their carers will always think the same way.) He is shrewd enough to acknowledge that, 'with this illness, logic doesn't come into it.'

Eventually, Eva found a private counsellor who succeeded in understanding and infiltrating her mind-set and in reversing the dangerous patterns of thought and behaviour which had permeated her illness.

The family don't regret sampling a wide range of treatments, and their story is testament to the idea that eating disorder patients and their families shouldn't be afraid to switch techniques if they feel that the path they're taking is not the correct one.

Eva's family were left in little doubt that, before finding the counsellor who hit upon an effective way to combat her illness, the treatments they tried were proving ineffectual. Josh was left with the impression that, while the professionals 'understood the illness on paper' they 'had no real empathy, no emotional connection to the sufferers,' which he has identified as 'vital when dealing with eating disorders.'

Many families do not have the confidence to take the decision favoured by the Mathers family and instead bow to what they perceive to be the superior knowledge of experts, persevering with ineffectual treatments. They do this for all the right reasons, because eating disorders are so incredibly difficult to comprehend from an outside perspective. Eating disorders are not like a broken leg, in which case the treatment is uniform and usually guaranteed to be successful. They require bespoke solutions, tailored to the sufferer.

Eva found her resolution in a 'treatment that was adapted to me, personally by someone I trusted'. Josh, Kyra and Charles are vocal about the importance of this bond of trust between patient and therapist. They all speak of Eva's counsellor being her 'Guardian Angel'.

Again, NLP and other alternative techniques were deployed in this instance. Kyra defines NLP as 'the best treatment' and again, as with Sam, emphasizes the importance of 'lots of patience and love'.

Josh brilliantly summarizes the experience of the entire Mathers family upon finding the right remedy for Eva when he says, 'It was like we could all finally breathe out after holding our breath for two years.'

Eva has now been in recovery for two years.

NATASHA'S STORY

It is not only anorexia which has a dramatic impact on the people within the sufferer's life. Bulimia is an illness that the average person wouldn't recognize unless they were looking for the very specific and subtle signs, and carers often feel completely isolated.

Natasha suffered from bulimia nervosa for eight years. Around two years into her illness, she realized she needed help and began seeking treatments. None of these treatments proved effectual until, aged 26, she underwent NLP and hypnosis. She's now been recovered for four years.

Initially, Natasha approached her GP at university, who 'actually shrugged'. She recalls, 'It was like he was saying, ''What would you like me to do?'' My illness escalated at that point.'

A free campus CBT service then provided some insight into Natasha's disorder. 'The campus counselling services were the first time I admitted to anyone the extent of my illness. From that point of view, they were useful.' CBT ultimately failed to rehabilitate Natasha, because:

> It became clear to me that my counsellor had never experienced an eating disorder as severe as mine before, and I began to get the impression she was using me as a case study. She would ask me to keep food/emotion diaries. When she read them, with raised eyebrows she'd exclaim 'Gosh!' before asking if she could keep them.

Natasha describes her desire to get better as 'coming in highs and lows.' She says,

> I'd make half-hearted attempts to see NHS counsellors and (after a 12-week wait) they'd make me recount everything that had ever gone wrong in my life ever, before declaring that it was little wonder I was depressed. I left feeling lower than when I went in.

Throughout the duration of her illness, Natasha was unsure about the extent to which her family were aware she was suffering from bulimia. Natasha's mother, however, says:

> Once Natasha's illness became serious, there was never any guesswork. I knew my daughter had bulimia and I was completely horrified. No matter how clever bulimics think they're being, in reality they can never cover up what they are doing. It's heart-breaking to have to listen to your child cook something for themselves and throw it all up again.

There is still almost no support for carers of bulimics. And it's hardly polite social chit-chat, is it? If someone says, 'How is your daughter?' you can't say, 'She's mentally ill, actually, and spends half her life with her head in the toilet.'

In retrospect, Natasha, now aware that in fact several members of her family knew about her disorder and were extremely worried, says:

My illness had made me so selfish, so utterly self-involved and so prone to navel-gazing, that I simply had no understanding of the impact I might be having on the people around me. I'd feel guilty, but it was a huge, all-encompassing, non-specific guilt. The kind of guilt that makes you feel like you've been punched in the stomach. I couldn't see a way free from that guilt – it didn't occur to me that I could make everyone's lives better simply by becoming well.

It was at this stage that a new person came into Natasha's life, her now step-father. Natasha's mother recalls,

He was able to approach the situation without guilt. This was so important. As a parent you blame yourself for absolutely everything that happens to your child, whether or not it is within your control. Not embarrassing my daughter was also a huge factor. Natasha was adamant with me that she didn't have a problem. She was deep in denial and because it's all about toilet-based functions and bodily fluids we developed a 'don't mention the war' mentality about it.

When I met my now-husband, he said, 'Wow. That's awful. Let's get it sorted.' Sometimes you need someone with an outside perspective to see the bigger picture.

Natasha remembers instinctively trusting this person who was, at the time, her mother's boyfriend, and opening up to him about her illness. She says, 'He listened. He sympathized. He didn't judge. He acknowledged my problem. He made me believe I could truly get better.'

Together, with behind-the-scenes help from Natasha's mum, they found an NLP clinic which provided the key to Natasha's recovery:

NLP was ideal for me because by this stage bulimia was nothing but a habit and I just wanted rid. It's not for everyone, but I knew why I'd become ill, I'd explored my emotions to the point that I was bored of talking about them. After three sessions of NLP and hypnosis, the world seemed different. The bingeing and purging slowed down to twice per week for about a fortnight. Then one morning I woke up and suddenly thought, 'What have I been doing? What was all that about?' When I think about my eating disorder now, it's as if it happened to a friend I was once really close to but never see anymore.

Natasha's mother adds:

A lot of what bulimics are looking for is acknowledgement. I work for a well-known helpline now and when people phone me and say, 'I have an eating disorder,' I say, 'Is that bulimia? Or anorexia? Or something else?' It's nearly always bulimia, and they seem so shocked and pleased that I put it first on the list. Anorexia is seen as 'the glamorous one', but what bulimics are doing to themselves, both physically and mentally, is just as dangerous.

As a piece of advice to other carers, Natasha's mum says, 'I think, given my time again, I would have confronted my daughter earlier. But that's easy to say in hindsight.'

Once again, Natasha's story is testament to the importance of communication. Although she continues to experience a few relatively minor residual health problems, Natasha is now healthy and 'infinitely happier than I was.'

CLAIRE'S STORY

The majority of the advice given to us with regard to weight loss recommends going to our GPs. The reaction of medical professionals to patients who over-eat is crucial. Compulsive and binge eating are often shrouded in denial and secrecy, so an acknowledgement of the problem and the desire to seek outside help is often difficult. Pride must be swallowed and realities checked. It's also tempting for the sufferer to attempt to rely on diet plans in magazines, on television or recommended by friends, and assume that the necessary changes can be made using willpower alone. As anyone who has ever dieted knows, this is invariably not that case. Compassion and a genuine understanding of the underlying issues are the cornerstones of obesity treatment.

Claire, who is 29 years old, approached her GP for weight loss guidance and was referred to the resident nurses. She says, 'I had tried so many ways to lose weight, so surely this had to help! No, would be the answer.'

Disappointingly, she found that the nurses concentrated solely on the physical aspects of her eating disorder, and then often with only a rudimentary understanding of nutrition. 'The only advice I got was not to eat Mars bars – Go figure! They gave me no real insight into healthy eating and meal ideas.'

Claire also recalls how she felt under immense pressure to lose a certain amount of weight each week. Obesity is characterized by feelings of shame and guilt, so to exacerbate these feelings by putting unnecessary pressure on a patient to reach certain weight targets can, ironically, promote a greater desire to eat.

In just the same way as anti-depressants are often perceived as a 'quick fix' for anorexics and bulimics by medical professionals, so diet pills were offered to Claire on three separate occasions, and she claims she was 'made to feel strange for refusing'. Claire believes that, had she accepted the diet pills, her weight loss would have been accelerated to the extent that she would have met the targets set for her by the nurses. She is not specific about how much she was asked to lose each week, but is of the opinion that diet pills would have been 'the only way you could possibly lose weight at the rate they wanted you to.'

While diet pills combat the physical symptoms of obesity, the underlying emotional issues remain, meaning relapse is likely, if not inevitable.

Claire's boyfriend Andy was a huge source of support to her, and instrumental in her recovery. He sums up his feelings during this time when he says:

*We had tried and tried and for so long I felt as if I was
between a rock and a hard place. I couldn't push for less food
or more exercise without the fear of causing a downward
spiral, ending with a beautiful woman feeling like she was
rubbish.*

Claire went on to find a counsellor who helped her address the
reasons underlying her over-eating. She says, 'You can't just
eat lettuce all day and expect the feelings to go away. It just
doesn't work like that. All the emotions are still there, under the
surface.'

Claire is careful to emphasize that she 'hasn't lost millions of
pounds', yet the transformation in her attitude and mind-set has
been staggering. She describes her food and exercise habits as
'sensible' now, and is losing her excess weight gradually and,
more crucially, safely. She says, 'Not only have I been able to
control my eating … I don't panic if friends want to go on a long
walk. Most of all, my home life is about happiness.' She cites
her counselling as the reason for 'knowing I have the strength
to continue on my path.'

Andy adds:

*Now, moving forward, we don't need to worry, as Claire
makes her decisions not on her size this week or the weight
she was last week. She makes what she thinks is a good
choice. I try to remind Claire that you don't have good or bad
food, you simply make an educated choice with the tools you
have at your disposal.*

For Claire the proof is, literally, in the pudding. She sums up her experience by saying, 'I look forward to my long and happy life. I can have pudding or not, whatever I feel like – go me!'

SUMMARY

As these stories show, just as no two sufferers are the same, no two paths to treatment are the same. As a carer you must not be afraid, if one form of treatment is not working for you and your loved one, to look for and try another which may work for you all. Debbie Roche, founder of the Plymouth-based eating disorder support group NotEDuk, whose son Ollie is in recovery from anorexia, summarizes her experience as a carer when she says:

> I know I would do exactly the same again. However, I would have more of an understanding of the complexities of anorexia nervosa. I would be more knowledgeable of the rights of sufferers and their families and I would begin to shout for necessary changes a great deal sooner.

In the next chapter we will explore the various treatments available, from the traditional to the cutting-edge, to give you an insight into how they work and what they do, and help you identify which ones may be suitable for you.

CHAPTER 5

A GUIDE TO THERAPIES

In order to be proactive during this frustrating time, one step which carers, parents and friends of sufferers can take is to arm themselves with a thorough knowledge of the various treatment options available. Both our family and the Mathers family stories in the previous chapter refer frequently to NLP, CBT, TFT and Bodytalk. These are all alternative therapies which have been shown to be effective in combating eating disorders. This chapter aims to provide you with everything you need to know about these treatments and others and their use in relation to eating disorders.

NLP

NLP is an acronym for neuro linguistic programming. This sounds complicated but isn't. 'Neuro' means mind, 'linguistic' means language and 'programming' refers to our patterns of thought and behaviour. So, in its simplest form, NLP aims to change our patterns of thought and behaviour by changing the language of our minds. The central idea isn't a new one – in fact the Bible advises us to 'be transformed by the renewal of your mind.'

In order to 'reprogram' the mind, NLP relies on a variety of techniques, including affirmations (repetition of positive statements), reframing (the practice of putting traumatic memories into a different context), anchoring (using a physical object or gesture to 'tune in' to positive memories and emotions) and hypnosis.

NLP works on the principle that the mind is 91 per cent unconscious (and therefore only 9 per cent conscious). If our brain were a warehouse, then the majority of 'storage space' would be in the unconscious mind. Rather brilliantly, therefore, any behaviour which we undertake on a regular basis is 'stored' in the larger unconscious, thus freeing our conscious mind to deal with those activities which require our full concentration.

The easiest way to demonstrate this phenomenon is using the example of driving. When a student first learns to drive, he or she is in a constant state of intense concentration. It seems impossible that clutch control, steering and observation can be mastered simultaneously – the student driver fears roundabouts, traffic lights, oncoming vehicles, pushbikes, pedestrians and essentially any stretch of road which isn't long, straight and hazard free. (It's therefore somewhat ironic that they aren't permitted to drive on motorways.)

After a few months or years, however, driving becomes automatic. We lose all conscious awareness of the thought mechanisms we employ in order to drive. Frequently, seasoned drivers arrive at their destination with no recollection of how they got there, particularly if it's a journey they undertake regularly. Their unconscious mind has relieved the conscious of the burden of having to remember how to drive.

In this instance the mechanism works to our benefit, but in others it can work to our detriment. So it is with eating disorders. Nathan, a former bulimia sufferer who attributes NLP to his recovery, says:

> *I was at this point where I knew what I was doing was harmful and I'd made the decision I wanted to stop, but somehow I couldn't. Every day was the day I was going to stop making myself sick. And yet this binge/purge compulsion took over and there I was with my head in the toilet.*

Nathan had been bulimic for a number of years (although it can take as little as a few weeks, for a habit to form and be adopted by the unconscious) and had made the decision he wanted to recover using his conscious mind (9 per cent), which was then attempting to take on the might of his unconscious mind (91 per cent). The unconscious will, by nature, persuade you to do what you have always done. This also happens with smokers, and it happens with those who attempt to diet and fail.

NLP is a technique which allows the therapist to infiltrate the more powerful unconscious mind and undo the harmful habits and thought patterns which have been formed. Essentially, however, it's the patient who wants to make the changes, and NLP wouldn't be effective if they did not.

Many people fear NLP, imagining that the therapist can fundamentally change your personality, or force you to act against your will. NLP isn't magic, however, and nothing can happen in a therapy session which the sufferer does not allow (both fortunately and unfortunately in the case of eating disorder patients).

NLP also focuses heavily on values and beliefs (both of which are omnipresent within the unconscious mind). Values are those things which are most important to us; however, they are metaphysical or conceptual. When asked to name the things which mean most to them, many people say their family or their house or their career. The idea which infuses their conviction that these things are important is the person's actual 'value'. So, for example, if a person values their house they have a need for security and routine. If a person values their career they have a need to be appreciated and rewarded for what they do.

The most common values are honesty, respect and fairness. When these are violated, in however small a way, they provoke a huge and often disproportionate reaction, a reaction which we frequently don't fully understand ourselves.

If a sufferer feels undervalued, unappreciated, disrespected or undermined, the eating disorder becomes a coping mechanism – and often the reaction is disproportionate. A throwaway comment or a seemingly insignificant incident (usually in childhood) which violates the sufferer's core values is often instrumental in fuelling the fire of their illness. NLP allows them to identify the incident, to recognize that their reaction was inappropriate or disproportionate, to forgive the perpetrator and to move on with their lives.

Beliefs differ from values, but are still a hugely potent force when determining the nature of how a patient thinks. Often, beliefs are referred to in NLP as 'mind chatter'. Highlighting and reversing a sufferer's negative mind chatter is crucial. Often the beliefs have little or no basis in reality. For example, if a sufferer has an older sibling who is more academically gifted than them, this might eventually convert to the belief that they are 'stupid'. This belief roots itself in the powerful unconscious part of the brain, and affects not only how sufferers perceive themselves, but also how they are perceived and the decisions they make throughout their lives.

Eating disorder patients regularly believe to the core of their being that they are in some way inadequate or unloveable. NLP works using affirmations and hypnosis to reverse this dangerous and self-perpetuating mind chatter.

Max Kirsten is a clinical hypnotherapist and NLP Master Practitioner who has had great success in treating bulimia and obesity using his techniques. He says:

> *Bulimia comes up a lot, but anorexia is the hardest eating disorder to treat. Anorexics go into the deepest holes and they don't want to come out. I've managed to make a few of them stop digging long enough to blink and to question whether they are doing the right thing, but I've not been able to get them out of their hole. They are the ones, who*

have to climb out of the hole themselves when they finally see the light.

However, as the family testimonials show, NLP and clinical hypnotherapy can often be used as a valuable element of a therapy course which encompasses many aspects in order to treat anorexics. Max agrees, 'I am willing to try all sorts of things as I think [with anorexia] one [treatment] modality is simply not enough.'

NLP and hypnotherapy have advantages over other treatments, in that modifications to the patient's mind-set can be made incredibly quickly. However, Max says, although he needs only three to five sessions to get a client on the right track, they 'need support or it won't work.' Some sufferers have this support network at home or among their peers, while others feel the need to touch base regularly with their valued and trusted therapist. Max says:

I have some clients I keep in touch with; if they begin to feel isolated ... they will usually begin to 'wobble'. There is an old saying that 'an addict alone is in bad company.' Sessions with me combined with intensive counselling would provide the ideal 'total immersion' in the recovery process and really help keep them on track.

Max identifies their process among other things as 'seeking comfort' and adds that, 'Simple yet powerful NLP anchoring techniques can be used [for comfort] throughout the day, for example breathing and posture to change their conscious state from feeling lack to feeling well, confident and complete.'

John Arroyo, also an NLP Master Practitioner, has worked with anorexics and has a high success rate. He says:

Using NLP tools and principles, the therapist can quite quickly establish how the client holds their anorexic patterns, strategies and mind-set, and then work directly with these patterns to change them and to teach the client how to think differently. The therapist can add flexibility and choice to the patient's thoughts, and learn new strategies and behaviours. This will give the client the psychological freedom and the true control they desire.

John has also used his method to treat obesity. He identifies over-indulgence with food as a coping mechanism for difficult emotions and says that, in this regard, compulsive eating is 'like any other eating disorder.'

NLP is concerned with identifying the root cause of destructive patterns of behaviour and, with obese clients, associations have often been made between food and 'reward', or food as 'medicine' for minor physical or emotional upsets. This happens during childhood, when 'treats' are proffered in response to academic achievements, good behaviour, grazed knees, trips to the doctor, etc. John says:

I have a client at the moment who ... remembers being upset when she was about eight years old and her mum buying her an ice cream. It made her feel better and since then she has been using food to make herself feel better.

When I first met her she told me she was walking down the street and someone called her a fat pig. It made her feel worthless, so she went to the bakers and bought herself

> *three bags of doughnuts. For two hours, the feelings of*
> *worthlessness were taken away, but then replaced by guilt for*
> *eating the doughnuts. To get rid of guilt she ate two large bars*
> *of chocolate … So the cycle continues.*

In this client's case, the aim of NLP was to provide her with the tools she needed to feel confident and worthy, without relying on food. John taught his client to 'use different strategies to manage uncomfortable feelings. By doing this she feels better and is losing weight.'

Essentially, NLP and hypnotherapy allow the sufferer to reconnect with the person they were before the eating disorder took hold, and to be liberated from the negative emotions which perpetuate harmful cycles of behaviour. Eating disorders are frequently tied up with feelings of guilt or insecurity and of low self-worth. Once these feelings have been relived so often, they form neural pathways in the brain, allowing us to freshly revisit traumatic and hurtful past experiences and to look for coping mechanisms long after the events have happened. NLP restores neural pathways to their natural state, allowing us to be the person we were meant to be. This is by no means a flawless person, but it is a person who doesn't wilfully damage themselves. Max Kirsten describes this process in his book *Self-Help: Find Your Self to Help Yourself* (Hay House, 2011) as 'becoming the person you want to be – taking care of yourself – learning to let yourself take care of you'.

Former bulimia sufferer Nathan concurs with this:

> *As I left my last NLP session, it was as if a huge weight had*
> *been lifted from my shoulders. I realized I was constantly*

feeling guilty and unloved. No wonder I sought solace in food and felt the need to punish myself by purging! The feelings were so omnipresent, I forgot they were there. But as soon as they were gone I could begin living my life again. I finally feel like me.

HYPNOTHERAPY

Largely owing to the way hypnosis is described and presented by the media, there's a great deal of myth and misconception surrounding it. As mentioned above, hypnosis is a key tool used by NLP practitioners, and allows fast and permanent changes to be made in the unconscious mind.

For a large majority, the word 'hypnosis' conjures up visions of magician-type performers persuading unwitting volunteers that they're a chicken/can fly/have an otter in their trousers. We're led to believe that hypnosis involves the total surrender of one's will to another person, who is then free to manipulate their hypnotised subject in any way they please.

In reality, hypnosis is simply a deep (and very pleasant) state of relaxation. When we awake on a Saturday or Sunday morning and have nothing to leap out of bed for, we tend simply to lie still and enjoy the sensation of being somewhere between sleep and total alertness. We'd still be able to jump to attention in the event of an emergency, and we're aware of the thoughts that drift in and out of our minds. It's this state which hypnosis exactly replicates.

Hypnosis works by 'shutting down' the conscious mind and directly accessing the larger and more influential unconscious. This is exactly what happens while we are sleeping. The conscious mind rests while the unconscious continues to work feverishly – unravelling and exploring the day's events through dreams.

When hypnotised, contrary to popular belief the subject is usually aware of everything the therapist is saying to them. They might, however, drift in and out of a light sleep. They will almost always believe that the hypnotherapy session has been much shorter than it was in reality (because they are so deeply relaxed, time appears to elapse faster). After hypnotism, the patient may feel euphoric or extremely tired. This is because the unconscious mind has been exerting itself, taking on information and initiating positive changes.

A good hypnotherapist will work with the client to establish the language they use in relation to the issue they want to change, and incorporate this into the therapy session. For example, if a compulsive eater says, 'When I start to binge, it's like I've boarded a train that won't stop,' the hypnotherapist will recognize that, in the mind of the sufferer, they think of a train whenever they binge. He or she can then work with that imagery and speak directly to the patient's unconscious.

Hypnotherapy uses imagery and language to place the patient in a fictitious environment where they feel safe and secure. This will vary with each person, although it's usually set in nature, for example on a beach or in a forest or meadow. The hypnotist will then work with the client to create scenarios designed to deal with their issues. For example, eating disorder sufferers who have had traumatic experiences in childhood will often harbour feelings of guilt and bitterness, which then infuse and spur on their behaviour. A hypnotherapist might encourage them to visualize a scenario in which they 'burn' something which represents their past (sometimes a pile of leaves), setting a new precedent within the brain and signalling that that portion of their life has now come to a close.

Juliette underwent hypnotherapy for compulsive eating. She attributes her condition to the destructive and emotionally abusive relationship she had with her step-father while growing up. She says:

During hypnosis I was imagining I was on a beach. My therapist asked me to write the initials of anyone who had ever hurt me in the sand. I immediately thought of my step-dad and drew his initials alone. [My therapist] then asked me to draw a circle around the initials and to take a few steps back. I then watched as the tide came in and washed away the circle and the initials. When I came out of hypnosis I felt utterly euphoric. I realized that the bitterness I felt towards my step-father had been like a millstone around my neck. That simple but incredibly potent exercise had liberated me. For the first time I felt entitled to eat healthily.

COUNSELLING

The word 'counselling' covers a multitude of different disciplines. Often counsellors will use an element of psychotherapy, CBT (see page 113) and NLP within their method. Most broadly, however, counselling offers an opportunity for patients to talk.

In an anonymous and safe environment, patients are afforded the opportunity to speak about anything, while being gently guided with questions by their therapist which allow them to come to important realizations about the origin and nature of their illness.

Counselling has a number of benefits for eating disorder patients. Firstly, it allows them to feel valued. Eating disorder sufferers, and in particular bulimics and binge eaters, often feel isolated and misunderstood. Counselling provides a forum for them to explore their feelings. Secondly, counselling is, by its very nature, tailored to the individual. There is no set format for counsellors, which means that they must, to some extent, treat every patient's case individually.

As such, it is crucial in counselling, perhaps more so than with any other type of therapy, to find the right fit in terms of a practitioner. A good counsellor should make their patient feel safe, secure and valued at all times. They should establish a bond of trust with their clients and make it easy for them to discuss potentially painful of difficult issues.

As an eating disorder counsellor, I ensure I have met with a sufferer's parents or carers before I commence working with them, if they are under 18. Many people are surprised that I insist on this. I have always been of the opinion, however, that rehabilitating an eating disorder sufferer is a group effort and one which will involve constant channels of communication between the patient and the people who are most influential in their life.

If a patient is over 18 and they have approached me independently, I will usually bring carers into the process a little further into therapy. Under the Data Protection Act, I of course have to gain the client's permission to share information with their carers. Once I have explained the paramount importance of trust and communication, this permission is usually granted.

I like the families of my patients to understand my methods and the work I will undertake with their loved one so that they can be helpful and supportive throughout the process. Recovery can sometimes be a long process, with the sufferer's mind-set changing at each stage, sometimes on a day-by-day basis. It's important that carers are aware of the changes to help them to gain a real insight into how their loved one is thinking and feeling at each juncture within the process. This is why I prefer to keep them in the loop.

Before a client sees me for the first time, I research their interests, whether it's films they enjoy or music they listen to, so that I can establish a rapport with them during their first session. It is important for sufferers to feel understood and accepted. It is also crucial that they perceive themselves as a three-dimensional person, rather than as simply 'an eating disorder'. Eating disorders envelop the identity of the sufferer. By talking to my clients about their hobbies and passions, I am demonstrating to them that they are individuals, who are not defined by their illness. This puts into motion the journey towards my client envisaging life without their issue – a huge leap in terms of the recovery process.

Encouraging clients to acknowledge their issue and open up about the factors which might have influenced it is not easy – it requires patience and perseverance. I work very intensively with my clients initially, seeing them two or three times per week. The challenge to negative emotions must be immediate and swift. We also establish a bond of trust and friendship during this time. Eventually this can be maintained with less frequent sessions.

Eva was one of my counselling patients. She says:

> *There are many words that come to mind when I think of the textbook treatment I received before discovering Lynn. 'Cold', 'emotionless' and 'detached' are some I could pick out. However when Lynn opened her heart and let me in, that's when the strength of hers healed mine. Words which come to mind when I think of the treatments that lead me back to my life again are 'hope', 'strength' and 'determination'.*

These sentiments are echoed by another of my clients, Chloe, who describes her depression as, 'The heavy, grey fog … that insidious, nagging voice of my inner critic.' She says that counselling left her 'brimming with optimism, ready to leap into the life I want and deserve … I am in control, I am free.'

Counselling is, ultimately, the client's journey and not my own. It is important that the people I work with look forward to their sessions. Each client's therapy is adapted to their individual requirements and needs, as I find this helps them to relax and feel more at ease, so enabling them to engage with me and make progress in their therapy. All the techniques I use help to reinforce a client's own desire to get better. If they do not have this desire, counselling may stabilize them but it cannot move them forward.

The most important consideration when embarking upon a course of counselling is that the therapist is the right 'fit' for the sufferer. Lori Henry recognizes this when remembering her own journey to recovery:

> I learned the importance of not just finding a therapist, but the right therapist. My therapist didn't focus on what I was eating and how many calories I was consuming, but dug deeper into why I felt so overwhelmed. Bulimia was a tool I reached out for to help me deal with my life, instead of dealing with the emotions I was feeling.

CBT

The aim of CBT is to allow patients to tackle damaging patterns in their thought processes and rationale using discussion-based therapy and by managing their behaviour.

Although well-established and empirically proven, CBT encompasses a number of different therapeutic systems which are tailored to the patient and their specific issue (making it ideal for eating disorder treatment, when sufferers are so often made to feel undervalued and disrespected). For example,

CBT often includes multimodal therapy (based on the idea that each of the body's various modalities – our ability to think, feel, sense, interact and imagine, for example – can be addressed using psychological treatment) and rational emotive behavioural therapy (a type of therapy inspired by modern philosophers to encourage patients to harness and take control of their feelings).

CBT can be incredibly effective for eating disorder sufferers who have difficulty relinquishing control – it encourages patients to shift the focus of their control to their behaviour and thought processes on a conscious level, using specific exercises. This allows them to be active in the entire process. For example, an obese patient may be told to put their knife and fork down for a pre-agreed number of seconds between each mouthful of food. This not only allows the patient to register when they are full and slow down the eating process (making it less likely to escalate into a binge), it also gives them a sense of jurisdiction over their eating habits.

CBT takes a 'one day at a time' approach, and can be used in conjunction with NLP to positive effect. It works on the basis that eating disorder recovery is a lengthy struggle, and equips the patient with the tools they need in order to tackle the everyday difficulties they might encounter.

Anorexics are prone to panicking in social environments and in any circumstances in which the consumption of food is expected or inevitable. CBT is particularly effective in allowing them to feel they have the ability to go about their lives without the fear of encountering these situations.

Sarah is a former anorexic. Although she is now able to eat healthily, she continues to use CBT in conjunction with other therapies in order to tackle the residual emotions her condition has left her with. She found that CBT was instrumental in her initial recovery.

Like many CBT patients, Sarah was asked to keep a food/emotion diary. This involves recording each meal and snack and how the sufferer feels before and after eating it. In this way, associations can be made by both client and therapist between certain emotional states and the subsequent desire either to eat or starve. Sarah says:

> *Being a bit of a control freak at times, I find it incredibly helpful if I can understand* why *I feel the way I do. By recognizing patterns in both my emotional and behavioural responses, I felt more able to begin to challenge these.*

Sarah is also vocal about the benefits of being able to explore daunting emotions and behaviours within the safe confines of her therapist's office:

> *Having the opportunity to revisit specific examples of distress and struggle with the space and distance from the original event, and to be more logical and rational, allowed me to begin to understand and pick apart exactly what had made that situation as stressful as it was. By doing this I became more aware of 'danger areas' that I was likely to slip up in, and could therefore begin to develop ways in which to help myself, should a similar situation occur. This ultimately gave me back some of the control that I had lost.*

Interestingly, when Sarah first began receiving CBT therapy she says she found it 'difficult to get on board with.' She attributes this to the fact that, in her warped eating-disordered logic, she had assumed that all her problems were due to food and how 'fat' she felt, when in fact what she did or did not eat was a direct response to the problems she had. She initially found it challenging to reverse this pattern of thought, but maintains that it is possible with 'perseverance'.

Sarah undertook some of her therapy in a group environment, which she reports as being very helpful: 'Hearing other people work through their emotional and behavioural patterns allowed me to relate myself to their examples and helped me to recognize patterns in my own emotional behaviour.'

At its most straightforward level, CBT is the practice of persisting in asking a patient, 'Why?' Often they cannot answer, but have at the very least been encouraged to embark on an internal dialogue, questioning their feelings and behaviour. Sarah recalls the following conversation between herself and her therapist, following a particularly challenging encounter with a pizza, which demonstrates this technique:

Therapist – Why are you feeling so frustrated and anxious?

Sarah – Because I feel disgusting and repulsive and huge.

T – Why?

S – Because I just ate pizza and I shouldn't have done it.

T – Why not?

S – It's too fattening and I can't afford to eat things that might make me bigger.

T – Why not?

S – Because I'm too fat anyway.

T – What would happen if it did make you put on weight?

S – I would be even fatter.

T – And what?

S – And I'll be embarrassed and even more ashamed.

T – Of what?

S – Because I will take up too much space.

T – And what?

S – And I don't deserve to.

T – Why not?

S – Because I will just get in the way ...

T – Who says?

S – Me.

T – Who else?

S – Loads of people.

T – Like who?

S – ... I, well, loads ...

T – Who?

S – ... I don't ... (after a long pause) I'm not answering because I'm not going to win this argument.

Joanne, a child psychologist, believes that there is a great deal of value in this 'And so what if …?' style line of questioning. She says:

> By saying to an anorexic patient, 'You won't get fat' you are colluding with the idea that fat is bad, the worst thing that could happen, fat must be avoided literally at all costs, and [you are] telling them that you agree with the premise that may well be at the root of their problem – rather than inculcating a balanced view of body size.

The logical conclusion is that CBT might allow an anorexic to see that there are worse things to be than overweight, by allowing them to explore in a safe environment the possible ultimate consequences of the things they most fear. However, since they are unlikely to become overweight in any case, and they, contrary to popular belief, are aware of this, the fear of food is removed altogether.

Sarah summarizes by saying, 'I strongly believe that, with eating disorders, food is the symptom and not the cause. It wasn't until I began using CBT techniques and exercises that I realized this.'

BODYTALK

Bodytalk is a holistic therapy, meaning that it is concerned primarily with the relationship between body and mind, but is not limited to this. Understanding the significance of the part the emotions play in a person's wellbeing, Bodytalk literally works on every level of the human being and excludes nothing.

Established in the mid-1990s by Dr John Veltheim, Bodytalk describes itself as an 'integrative system' which taps into the 'innate wisdom' of the body to determine health problems that may be present and to treat them. Dr Veltheim has a background in acupuncture and chiropractic, and has developed the Bodytalk system to include the best the West has to offer married with the wisdom of Eastern practices.

Bodytalk hinges on the philosophy that the body is comprised of various energy systems designed to work in harmony. During periods of sickness – physical, mental or emotional – these energies can be enormously compromised, resulting in a complete imbalance in one or all of these areas.

While this might seem a little 'alternative' for some, the success of Bodytalk as an element of eating disorder treatment is undeniable. This might be because the sufferer is encouraged to establish a bond of trust with their body once more so, just like NLP, they take responsibility for their own health. In eating disorder patients, the mind and body are at war, so Bodytalk is primarily attempting to open paths of communication between them, hopefully bringing harmony back to the partnership.

Kyra Mathers, whose daughter Eva was a client of mine, has gone on to train as a Bodytalk practitioner. She has an unshakeable conviction in the effectiveness of the therapy for treating eating disorders.

Kyra cites one of the benefits of Bodytalk as the fact that the patient does not have to identify their issues themselves. A skilled Bodytalk practitioner is able to establish areas of the body–mind complex that are out of balance and re-establish harmony within them. Often, in the initial stages at least, eating disorder patients are reluctant to open up and discuss their lives and habits with, for example, a counsellor, yet with Bodytalk, 'You don't have to speak at all if you don't want to.'

Of course, Bodytalk may 'throw up an issue which then needs to be dealt with' (these are likely to be psychological elements of the sufferer's condition). The patient may then need to go on to use a different therapy in conjunction with Bodytalk. Kyra is of the opinion that NLP is a particularly effective companion therapy for Bodytalk, so that the body and mind are targeted simultaneously.

She summarizes by saying, 'In hindsight, Bodytalk helped alleviate the stress, improve the mood, so enabling Eva to respond more effectively to her counselling.'

Laura Forbes is a Bodytalk practitioner who believes the therapy to be cutting-edge, describing it as 'one of the only truly holistic forms of bodywork in the world today.' Practitioners are trained to identify 'energy blockages' in the body which signify ill-health within the 'physical, emotional, mental and spiritual layers of the human make-up.' In this way, Bodytalk could be described as a 'blend of Eastern and Western philosophies' so creating a powerful therapy.

Laura has used Bodytalk to treat eating disorder patients, but concedes that it is most effective when used 'alongside other types of therapy in a team approach to recovery.' She adds, 'It is widely recognized that [eating disorders] are linked to control, which Bodytalk can help to balance, as well as establishing the reasons for this need.'

TFT

Ian Graham was one of the first practitioners to champion TFT and its use in the UK.

He summarizes the practice as a 'drug-free and largely talk-free therapy that can resolve many emotional and psychological problems by stimulation of acupressure points on the head, upper body and hands in a precise coded sequence.'

Tony Ford is an accredited practising counsellor who uses TFT in conjunction with counselling, when appropriate, when working with clients who are suffering with eating disorders.

As a counsellor I have found TFT to be useful and effective on occasions when working with clients with an eating disorder where compulsion and trauma have been present. First of all, an understanding of how an eating disorder evolves and takes hold can be very useful and plays an important role for the sufferer.

What is TFT?

TFT is based on the principle of muscle-testing and 'tapping' to treat problems, but is designed to rapidly break the link between one's thoughts and the triggering of any negative emotions that go with them.

The particular 'tapping' points on the body are found on the classical meridians discovered by the ancient Chinese and used in traditional Chinese medicine. The founder of TFT, Dr Roger Callahan, found that tapping on the meridian points in a specific order while the patient thinks about their problem deactivates what he calls 'perturbations' in the thought field. Callahan considers these to be the generators of the negative emotions associated with a certain situation or experience.

TFT works on the basis that there are set programs within the human mind and body for each emotion, although our responses to them vary wildly. For example, anger manifests itself as the same pattern of emotion in everyone, but while some repress their anger, others become tearful and others violent. TFT claims to intercept the pathway between our thoughts about a triggering situation and the emotional response, in cases where the response is excessive or inappropriate.

Tony Ford points out that it is also important to understand the correlation between disproportionate emotion and damaging behavior, and why understanding the reasons behind this can help consolidate the positive effects of TFT.

Having worked with clients presenting an eating disorder, psychological distress is at the heart of their difficulty in trying to establish a healthy diet and weight. This distress can be varied in its origin and yet have similar characteristics: from arguments at the dinner table to more extensive and damaging origins such as various unhealthy attachment experiences and distortions.

Although there is no empirical evidence for TFT, for eating disorder patients its theoretical workings provide a very plausible solution. In a binge eater, for example, the default response to difficult emotions such as stress, loneliness or boredom is to eat. If the process can, as Ian Graham maintains, break the 'coded link between thought and action', it can allow patients to retain thoughts and memories of triggering situations but, in the absence of the negative emotional response, react in a different way. Ian also points out that the process can lead to a reversal of behaviour in binge eaters – for whom, often 'the thought of food triggers the fear of not getting food.' He believes TFT can negate that fear so the individual need no longer respond to it by over-eating.

Ian cites food addiction as the eating disorder that TFT is most effective in treating, but believes it can be used in conjunction with other therapies as part of a program to combat anorexia and bulimia. As with Tony Ford, Ian is wary of recommending TFT as a full and final solution for eating disorders, but believes that it can definitely help. Tony Ford notes that, 'In my experience it is often a combination of expression and application through applicable and achievable steps which gets results.' Tony has used TFT in particular when working with clients who have experienced trauma. He says:

These difficult past experiences can resurface through similar external situations and experiences. These unresolved past events could cause a triggering effect. Triggers for disordered eating can be surprisingly simple and mundane. However, where trauma has occurred, TFT can help the previously held emotion to the event to be released. With any TFT treatment, especially in conjunction with an eating disorder, a mindful exploration and understanding is vital to bring awareness to the coping behaviour.

What's more, as Ian Graham points out, 'TFT can empower the sufferer to limit their emotional trauma. [It] can help reduce the emotional sequelae that go with the [eating] disorder. Anxiety, anger, shame and guilt can all be quickly and painlessly resolved.'

What sets TFT apart from other therapies is that clients are taught to use the technique on themselves. They are shown the various meridian points which must be tapped. In this way, sufferers are less likely to become dependent on their therapist. It is essential with eating disorder sufferers that they realize that the person most instrumental in their recovery is themselves. They cannot be allowed to believe that their therapist has done the work for them, as this increases the chance of relapse when they encounter difficult situations in the wider world. TFT equips clients with the expertise to treat themselves as and when they require it, so that they can maintain considerable autonomy and control over their own recovery process. As Tony Ford says:

People suffering from an eating disorder often feel restricted in their mind and subsequent behaviour. TFT is another foot hold to autonomy: to apply and promote healthy mindful behaviour, with how they feel, not just only around food but more importantly about their feelings towards the self.

Ian Graham adds, 'TFT is quick, but it is not a quick fix. Client commitment and investment in their future is essential.'

DBT

DBT is an acronym for 'dialectical behaviour therapy'. DBT has its origins in CBT and is similar in many ways. However, it differs in that it is designed to suit patients who have been diagnosed with borderline personality disorder or another mental health issue which is not directly linked to their eating disorder (and are therefore less likely to respond to traditional CBT).

DBT is concerned exclusively with treating obstructive and dangerous patterns of behaviour. It does not search for, nor attempt to address, the emotional origins of an eating disorder. It is therefore only usually recommended for a specific type of patient for whom delving into their past to explore their emotions might prove counterproductive.

Lottie is a recovering anorexic. She believes that DBT helped her overcome her tendency to 'mentally tot up calories or plan what I would have for dinner, rather than participating in exercises.'

As with Sarah's experience of CBT, Lottie was asked to keep a food diary. She worked with a nutritionist in addition to a DBT practitioner over a period of 18 months to ensure she would complete her exercises and not give in to the temptation to relapse.

She says, 'DBT was hard work and progress was slow. It required immense commitment. Although it did not completely eradicate my self-harming or disordered eating, the evidence from my diary suggests these behaviours significantly reduced whilst in DBT.'

GASTRIC BAND

A gastric band is a serious medical procedure which involves the patient having their stomach 'stapled', reducing its size so that it can then only take a small amount of food (usually just a couple of spoonfuls).

Gastric bands are a last resort of overweight patients who cannot seem to stop eating using more conventional methods. Beverley, who underwent the operation, says she had tried to lose weight 'every which way you could think of. I joined every slimming club. I tried private diet clinics (who gave me appetite suppressants) and weight-loss drinks.'

Beverley claims that her weight left her clinically depressed and house-bound before the operation. She opted to have a gastric band fitted privately, at a cost of £6,000. While she has since dropped five dress sizes, and says that her gastric band was

'100 per cent successful, re my weight loss', she does not feel that undergoing the procedure has changed her mind-set at all.

And therein lies the biggest pitfall of the gastric band (aside from the potential medical complications during surgery). It does not re-educate the over-eater, it does not allow them to love themselves and treat their body with respect. It focuses solely on the physical symptoms of over-eating. Beverley says:

Fifteen months on I still have bad eating habits, though the band restricts my intake. My mind-set is still the same. I still want to eat like the big girl before the op. I look in the mirror and still see a fat girl.

Gastric bands can be highly effective in treating morbidly obese patients who risk serious illness or even death because of the strain their weight is placing on their health. However, it is not a 'quick fix' and should ideally be embarked upon alongside some form of psychological treatment, such as counselling, to combat the underlying emotional issues fuelling the patient's desire to over-eat.

GASTRIC MIND BAND

The 'Gastric Mind Band' was invented and pioneered by leading hypnotherapist Martin Shirran. Using a combination of hypnotherapy, CBT and NLP, a combination of treatment Martin describes as 'Life Architecture', the therapy promises to help over-eaters reprogram their mind and create their own food rules.

The Gastric Mind Band places the utmost importance on 'eating mindfully', which we touched upon in Chapter 2. This is the act of concentrating solely on the food being consumed, not allowing distractions (such as television) to detract from the act of eating. The over-eater is taught to 'eat slowly and to cherish each and every mouthful' focusing on 'quality rather than quantity'.

The Gastric Mind Band takes place over the course of four sessions, and has a success rate of 75 per cent. It avoids all the possible medical complications of a traditional gastric band and, Martin says, 'enables the client to become the architect of their own life.'

Pearl underwent Gastric Mind Band therapy at Martin's clinic in 2011. Her story is familiar, in that she saw food as controlling her life previous to undergoing treatment, and had yo-yo dieted throughout her life. She considers her Gastric Mind Band to be an unequivocal success, saying:

The treatment worked immediately. At first I was very conscious of incorporating all of the mental and practical tools they gave me, but it quickly became a game and now is almost unconscious. It is empowerment. I am in control. Food does not control me. This is huge.

SUMMARY

Last year I watched a television programme in which the voiceover stated, as if it is fact, 'eating disorders are treated with a combination of anti-depressants and counselling.' This chapter has proved that not to be the case. There are a vast variety of treatments available for eating disorder sufferers, some of which may prove more effective than others for you and your loved one.

There is no 'correct' path to recovery. You may find a combination of treatments works best for you. The important thing to remember is that there is, without doubt, a form of treatment out there which can help your loved one as they return to health and happiness.

If one treatment is not working, do not be afraid to change tack and try another. As the testimonials in this book demonstrate, it is rare to stumble upon the perfect treatment first time round. Your loved one showing a willingness to get better is a huge step forward, and sometimes it can be frustrating when there is a delay in finding an effective treatment – I hope that this chapter has assisted you in making sense of some of the terms, buzzwords, etc. and will aid you in making an informed decision about what to try next.

At the back of this book you will find an index of resources and practitioners I have personally worked with, researched and/ or spoken to at great length about the treatments and methods they offer.

CHAPTER 6

COMPLEMENTARY THERAPIES

Complementary therapies can be used alongside orthodox medicine and counselling to increase the effectiveness of a programme of eating disorder treatment.

The NHS has experienced persistent and increased demand to incorporate complementary therapies over the past ten years. While many are scientifically impossible to validate, they unanimously place emphasis on providing a feeling of calmness, being more in control, reducing levels of stress and thereby boosting self-esteem.

Calmness, genuine control and self-esteem are exactly what is lacking in the life of an eating disorder sufferer. The value of complementary therapy is that it provides support for eating disorder sufferers on an emotional, mental, physical and spiritual basis, allowing them to direct their energies into something which has positive and affirming principles.

Alison Fuller, a holistic therapy practitioner, adds:

Sometimes simply being more open to holistic treatment enables us to perceive the benefit, albeit perhaps of a subtle nature, and it is this receptivity that allows shift and change to occur naturally, the impact of which can be boundary-less!

Carers can also feel the benefit from these treatments as they help to alleviate the stress associated with the emotional and physical demands that caring for someone with an eating disorder can bring.

As discussed in the previous chapters, it is essential for parents and carers of eating disorder sufferers to be both physically and mentally well and to enable them to take an active role in the patient's recovery.

Complementary therapies promote rest, relaxation and positive thinking – which are essential to any carer and can act as a valuable support during this difficult, stressful and emotionally draining time.

Below is a brief guide to various therapies and the benefits they potentially provide for both sufferers and the people around them.

REFLEXOLOGY

Reflexology is the technique of applying gentle pressure to specific areas on the feet to bring about a state of deep relaxation, stimulate the body's own healing processes and help the body return to a state of balance and wellbeing (homeostasis). It is excellent for restoring digestive order and hormonal balance.

The treatment helps to correct imbalances in bodily systems, thus restoring the body's natural healing power. A sequence is followed over both feet which incorporates all the organs, systems and meridians within the body, providing a totally holistic approach to wellbeing.

ACUPUNCTURE

Acupuncture is now becoming widely known and accepted. Its origins go back several thousand years and are based on the principle of energy, *qi*, flowing around the body via lines, channels or meridians and associated points along these lines. The meridians are associated with organs and systems of the body and should, ideally, be in a state of balance and flow. However, our lifestyles have an impact on our wellbeing, and ultimately we can suffer from poor health, pain and illness as a result.

Acupuncture is applied through the use of very fine needles inserted in points along the meridians with the aim of stimulating, reducing or moving energy to create flow and re-balance.

DEEP ABDOMINAL MASSAGE

Deep abdominal massage works the fascia (a layer of fibrous tissue) and connective tissue in the abdominal area to help the recipient unwind and to reduce stress and tension to the digestive and reproductive organs.

Carrying stress in the abdominal region can cause hormonal imbalance, weakness of the gut, blockage and restriction as well as discomfort. Increasing the flow of bodily fluids (i.e. blood, lymph, toxins and waste) helps to promote healthy tissue and organs, and improve digestive flow. It is therefore ideal for bulimics, who often experience pain and other medical problems in this region of the body. It has also been shown to aid problems with the female reproductive organs, which might be of benefit to former anorexics.

INDIAN HEAD MASSAGE

Commonly practised in India for over a thousand years, head massage is designed to alleviate stress and promote emotional tranquillity. Increasing circulation to the head has a number of physical benefits. By stimulating and massaging the hair follicles, Indian head massage can potentially assist hair growth, and encourage clear thinking and concentration. More importantly, the potential benefits of Indian head massage include relieving depression and reducing insomnia, which are widespread side-effects in all forms of eating disorders for both the sufferer and the carers alike.

REIKI

Reiki is a hands-on therapy facilitating deep levels of relaxation, stress relief, energy renewal and healing. The Japanese words *rei* and *ki* together mean 'divinely guided life force energy'.

Reiki restores balance to the body's vital energy, allowing the recipient to absorb what they need. Healing takes place on the physical, mental, emotional and spiritual level. The therapist places their hands on the clothed client and the energy flows where it is most needed, allowing the client to relax to the point of falling asleep.

The ultimate aim of Reiki is to bring about a calm and meditative state and a sense of emotional and spiritual wellbeing.

MASSAGE

Relaxing forms of massage aim to help the body heal itself and to increase health and wellbeing. Massage is known to be extremely beneficial in providing welcome relief from the symptoms of many ailments. It is a great relaxation therapy and can ease tension, anxiety and stress, symptoms that are present in many serious illnesses. It can also help with insomnia and depression.

Massage eases muscular tension and helps with back pain, headaches, joint pain, stiffness and even some forms of chronic pain. It is also known to stimulate the nerves and increase blood flow and circulation.

Regular massage treatments provide an excellent 'feel-good' factor as they are relaxing and de-stressing as well as being re-energizing and stimulating. They therefore help prevent the build-up of tension, anxiety and stress.

YOGA

A gentle form of exercise, yoga has a myriad of spiritual
and physical benefits and is practised throughout the world.
Rebecca Whitford has taught yoga for 12 years. She cites the
benefit of yoga for eating disorder patients as being the fact that
it:

*Gives you 'permission' to look after yourself, by listening to
your needs and responding to them. It is about accepting
who you are and tuning in to 'you'. A gentle class, with the
emphasis on relaxation, meditation and breathing, helps to
relieve both mental and physiological states such as anxiety,
to plant the seed of self-acceptance, relieve stress through
visualization and learn to be compassionate to oneself.
Someone with an eating disorder could definitely be helped
[with yoga].*

For compulsive exercisers, yoga is a way to exercise that is
'safe'. While an alcoholic cannot drink, exercise is universally
acknowledged to be a necessary part of health, so gentle
alternatives to cardiovascular and gym-based exercise needs to
be sought, and yoga is often the answer.

Rebecca advises:

*A teacher with an awareness of eating disorder issues would
be best, to teach the student not to force the body but to
accept its limitations. [An eating disorder patient] should go
to a class that is non-competitive ... with the emphasis on
moderation, balance and harmony.*

SUMMARY

Carolyne Cross, Vice Chair of the British Association of Beauty Therapy and Cosmetology (BABTAC), says:

> *It's no surprise ... that holistic treatments can have highly positive psychological effects on a client. The sense of wellbeing a client can experience from a treatment can go a long way in building and strengthening a client's self-esteem and thus having positive effects on one's health.*

The willingness of a sufferer to engage with complementary therapies shows that they are seeking positivity and a way to conquer their illness. This is one of the most crucial and valuable steps towards recovery.

For the carer, treatments provide respite in the form of a time-out to help renew their strength emotionally and physically and to enable them to face the challenges that they deal with, in their role as a carer for someone with an eating disorder.

I cannot reiterate enough that everyone is different and if one therapy does not work for you, don't be afraid to try another.

This chapter has provided only a brief description of each therapy. Full details of the therapists mentioned above are provided in the Resources section at the back of the book.

And what of the end of the journey, when your loved one has made their recovery? Where does that leave you, as their carer? I should stress, here, that it is very common and completely normal to feel mixed emotions at that stage. Your life, which has previously been dominated by your loved one's illness, might feel a little empty. Kyra summarizes this beautifully with the following analogy:

Being a carer to an anorexic felt like I was stranded at sea. I was on the boat and my daughter had fallen overboard. Eventually, I swam out and got a life jacket to her and we trod water for what seemed like an eternity, in the dark, not knowing when daylight would come. Eventually the sun came out again and we swam ashore. My daughter skipped off into the sunset and I was left, bedraggled, and never wanting to go on that boat again.

CHAPTER 7

INTERVIEW WITH JANET TREASURE

Professor Janet Treasure PhD FRCP PRCPsych is one of the world's leading experts in eating disorder research. In partnership with the Succeed Foundation (whose work we will explore in Chapter 14) and The South London and Maudsley Hospital and Kings Academic Partners in London, Professor Treasure undertakes pioneering research to help us to understand eating disorders and how to tackle them effectively.

Professor Treasure, who has written numerous books with practical tips for both eating disorder sufferers and carers (details of which can be found in the Resources section) has, throughout her career, been careful to emphasize the importance of carers in facilitating a sufferer's journey to recovery. She has also looked extensively at the most common (but natural and understandable) mistakes made by carers, as well as simple techniques they can learn to open channels of communication with their loved one, and aid them during the recovery process.

According to Professor Treasure's extensive back catalogue of research, there are three 'layers' within an eating disorder:

1. causal factors

2. further deterioration of the brain and thought processes (brought on by malnutrition)

3. the reaction to the illness by the people surrounding the sufferer

Professor Treasure believes that the initial causes of eating disorders are a combination of genetic make-up and environmental factors. Her research has revealed that our experiences in early life, including physical stress or trauma while in the womb, or during childbirth, can play a part in the onset of anorexia. In addition, Professor Treasure has found that there are some personality traits which lend themselves to an eating disordered mind-set. She describes a couple of the most common of these:

We have found that some anorexics would register mildly on the autistic spectrum. They are rigid and rule-bound in their thinking. These eating disorder patients have an attention to, and obsession with, detail which often renders them unable to see the bigger picture. Of course, in certain circumstances this can be a gift, but it is not so in anorexia.

Alternatively, some eating disorder patients are very concerned with competition and reward. They do not have the natural ability to be soothed simply by social interaction (which most of us have). They seek approval by achieving and through action, believing that it is the only way that they will be loved. They're also very sensitive to social rank.

This is not to suggest that an eating disorder is inevitable for anyone, however these types of personality are more predisposed towards eating-disordered thinking. Similarly, these personality traits can arise from an eating disorder, as opposed to triggering it. So, someone who has never displayed a particular attention to detail, for example, might suddenly become more rigid and detail-orientated after becoming trapped in anorexic ways of thinking.

Professor Treasure also recognizes that social factors can herald the beginnings of an eating disorder. In an earlier chapter we briefly discussed 'orthorexia', which arises out of a desire to emulate a 'fashionably' thin or chiselled body type. Professor Treasure concedes that any type of disordered relationship with food – such as fasting and feasting – can then lead onto 'phase two' of an eating disorder, in which the brain is unable to function. This second 'layer' of an eating disorder is the further obstacle to recovery, arising from starvation of the brain. Professor Treasure explains:

The brain is a highly vulnerable organ. It requires seven times more calories than any other body part in order to function properly. When it is starved, it interrupts logical thinking, which triggers the secondary changes in the sufferer.

The third layer of an eating disorder is the reaction of external parties to the sufferer and their illness. The way a sufferer's condition is reacted to has a huge effect in either facilitating, or setting back, recovery. Many of the errors carers make are both natural and logical, and in any other circumstances would be a sign of excellent parenting. That is why it is crucial to be educated in this regard, and to avoid common pitfalls.

Professor Treasure advises carers to be wary of conflict:

Don't charge in for a confrontation. At this stage, even a little opposition can force the sufferer further into denial. They will be adamant that they don't have a problem, and they will fool themselves into believing what they say.

Instead, Professor Treasure suggests opening up channels of communication with other people in the sufferer's life and, together, coming up with a list of evidence. This has two benefits – firstly, you can compare notes on the sufferer's behaviour and share ideas and reflections within the family or their friendship group. Secondly, when the time does come to discuss the situation with the sufferer, you have a logical response to their inevitable denial, which should prevent any emotionally driven screaming matches!

The most frequent error carers make, in Professor Treasure's experience, is to place the focus on food when approaching recovery. This is the most obvious thing to do, since you are, after all, dealing with an *eating* disorder. However, as we have seen in previous chapters, eating disorders are only a symptom of a deeper problem. 'Bear in mind that there are always deeper things underlying an eating disorder,' says Professor Treasure. 'Try to be sympathetic towards the anxiety and stress your loved one is experiencing.'

It is important to bear in mind that eating disorder sufferers are ultra-sensitive to criticism. Professor Treasure conducted some research with patients, showing them a series of human faces, some registering happiness, others disapproval. She found that the eating disorder patients would naturally focus on the disapproving faces and ignore totally the ones showing more positive emotion. In the same way, any criticism you level at or even suggest to your loved one will be exaggerated in their mind and potentially used as fuel for their illness.

Professor Treasure says that this is particularly an issue with bulimics and over-eaters, and their carers. Whereas an anorexic often inspires over-protection in the people around them (as they look and seem so frail), it can prove difficult for carers to maintain their patience with someone who binges. Bulimia is also messy, which can irritate the people the sufferer is living with. It's important always to acknowledge that bulimics and over-eaters are just as vulnerable as anorexics, and that their condition should be treated with just as much compassion and understanding.

Professor Treasure advocates using a technique known as 'motivational interviewing'. Her facility offers carers workshops which teach them how to use this strategy; essentially this involves communicating with the sufferer without judgement or criticism, but instead focusing on positivity and understanding. By avoiding criticism, the carer will find that their loved one will be more inclined to open up to them, establishing those all-important channels of communication.

Motivational interviewing involves what Professor Treasure describes as 'lashings of affirmation'. She notes that 'parents, in particular, often see their role as that of dishing out advice, which is then to be followed. This is not always helpful. Motivational interviewing encourages both parties to see the conversation from the perspective of the other.' In this way, not only does the carer have more genuine empathy with the sufferer, but the sufferer is encouraged to return the favour and attempt to see the situation from their carer's point of view. This is of particular value because, usually through no fault of their own, eating disorder sufferers are unable to see the consequences of their actions on the people around them.

For parents, Professor Treasure stresses that it is crucial to have a unified approach:

> *Often, I find that mothers are overprotective, whereas fathers tend to be mystified by eating disorders to a greater degree, so their natural reaction is to take a step back. You might think that this offers some kind of balance, but in fact it is a recipe for disaster. The important thing is that all the people dealing with the sufferer have the same understanding of their illness, and have agreed on their approach to it.*

It is also important for carers to communicate freely with medical professionals:

> *The medical community should share their knowledge with carers, as well as being honest about what they don't know. One of the biggest errors made by doctors is to take the view that they are breaking confidentiality if they communicate with a sufferer's parents or guardians once the [sufferer is] over the age of 18. It is not breaking a confidentiality to share their knowledge of the illness generally, or to teach carers*

techniques for dealing with it. They cannot go into specifics, but that does not mean that they cannot talk to carers at all.

Of course, eating disorder patients often encourage disunity between their friends/family and the medical professionals in their lives. This is for one of two reasons, in Professor Treasure's opinion. It might be because the sufferer is labouring under the misconception that their carers don't know, or indeed wish to know, about the extent of their illness, and they cannot bear the thought of being a burden to them by making them privy to that knowledge. The other, more sinister explanation is that anorexics, in particular, wish to 'divide and conquer'– they are aware, on an unconscious level, that their carers and therapists are stronger when taking a unified approach, so they use a distancing technique to allow themselves to stay sick.

The deviousness employed by anorexics is a trait of their illness, and is not who they really are. It is crucial to separate the characteristics of the eating disorder from the person who is suffering.

It's hard to reconcile the often tiny frame of an anorexic with our idea of a bully, and yet Professor Treasure has seen the ways in which carers are bullied by sufferers on numerous occasions during her career. Like all bullies, an eating disorder must be shown strength. Because sufferers are jeopardizing their own health, they often believe they have the ultimate 'trump card'. It is important to be strong enough to call their bluff.

As a carer, it's incredibly easy to allow aspects of yourself to slip away, as you attempt to deal with an eating disorder. Little by little, the illness takes over your life, as well as that

*of the sufferer. You may isolate yourself and stop going out,
or having friends to your house, either because it is too
difficult to explain what you are going through, or because the
sufferer does not like to be in mixed company. You may find
yourself walking on eggshells, terrified that you will do or say
something that will make their illness worse.*

It's equally important not to 'enable' the sufferer's illness, for an
'easy life': 'You might find yourself cleaning up after a bulimic,
for example, because you don't want them to be upset by the
mess they have made, but you're also preventing them from
seeing the consequences of their actions.'

During the course of her research, Professor Treasure has
observed three main caring styles, each totally natural and
understandable, but with unforeseen negative consequences
for the sufferer: she has termed these the Rhino, the Jellyfish
and the Kangaroo.

The Rhino

The Rhino charges into the situation, reasoning that they are
confronting and thereby solving it. This technique often proves
ineffectual, however, as it encourages the sufferer to defend
themselves and to be drawn deeper into their denial. It also
often causes arguments and disputes, which are upsetting for
all concerned.

The Jellyfish

The Jellyfish is emotional by nature and this will be evident
in their behaviour as a carer. They will often cry and shout,

emphasizing the effect the eating disorder is having on them, in the hope that the sufferer will see the error of their ways. However, just like their seafaring alter-ego, the jellyfish approach carries a sting – not only will the carer encourage their loved one to mirror their behaviour with dramatic outbursts, but they will further exacerbate the feelings of guilt and shame which characterize the sufferer's condition.

The Kangaroo

The Kangaroo is overprotective. They believe they are taking control of their loved one's issue and protecting them from the potentially harmful influence of the outside world, however they succeed in isolating the sufferer as well as themselves.

Professor Treasure recommends, instead, using more positive ways of caring, summed up by the Dolphin and the Saint Bernard.

The Dolphin

The Dolphin gently nudges the sufferer in the right direction, without being overbearing.

The Saint Bernard

The Saint Bernard is a constant companion, providing comfort, stability and love, but without interfering.

Professor Treasure emphasizes that the medical professionals she works with do recognize how difficult it is to be a carer to an eating disorder sufferer:

It's exhausting! Nurses can often get burn-out and they are only dealing with the illness in eight-hour shifts. The average length of time for an anorexic to suffer is 7 years, and a bulimic is 12 years. With other illnesses we are used to them being short term and having a fixed solution. With eating disorders you are often, sadly, in it for a long haul. We do recognize this and at Guys we offer workshops for carers to help them deal with and manage the situation.

Clinical depression and anxiety among carers is common, understandable and normal. However, Professor Treasure is quick to point out that these are usually short-term and that 'eventually, most carers feel that they have gained something from their experiences.' (In Chapter 6 we explored some alternative therapies which may help you to deal with and combat feelings of anxiety and depression in the short term.)

Professor Treasure echoes my beliefs that, when it comes to effective caring, patience, love and communication are the most important tools at our disposal. She also demonstrates the willingness of some people within the medical community to recognize the plight of carers and their fundamental role in the recovery process.

CHAPTER 8

MEN GET EATING DISORDERS TOO

In 2009 Sam Thomas, a former bulimia sufferer set up a website called 'Men Get Eating Disorders Too' (MGEDT, http://mengetedstoo.co.uk). The idea was that a demographic of male sufferers, who Sam was convinced had been overlooked by the medical community and the media, should have a forum to discuss their concerns and experiences in a mutually supportive environment. The response was overwhelming.

Male sufferers throughout the globe came forward, relieved and delighted to have the opportunity to be acknowledged at last. The website inevitably caught the attention of the local and national media, who began running stories on eating disorders among men as though they were an entirely new phenomenon.

The truth is, of course, that male eating disorders have been present within society for as long as their female counterparts, and yet there is undoubtedly a greater conspiracy of silence surrounding them.

The reasons for this are numerous. Men tend to communicate in an entirely different way to women within their peer groups. Body image and food issues are not generally discussed (whereas among women they are dissected and evaluated, often to the point of tedium). When a woman develops an eating disorder, she might feel isolated, but she will know with certainty that she is not alone. She will also know, to some degree at least, that her experiences replicate those of millions of women throughout the globe. Before Men Get Eating Disorders Too and other similar campaigns, men enjoyed no such comfort.

Eating disorders are often presented as a female-only issue. When we discuss them there is an assumption that the sufferer is a woman. Imagine someone said to you, 'My friend has anorexia.' The resultant visual image will probably be a female one. While it is true that, statistically, women are still more likely to suffer from an eating disorder, this could of course be because male sufferers are still less inclined to come forward and acknowledge the issue.

Eating disorders are still, somewhat misguidedly, associated solely with a preoccupation with one's appearance. We will explore throughout this and the next few chapters to what extent this is and is not true. The motivations for eating disorders are complex and manifold. This appears still not to be common knowledge, leading to the assumption that eating disorders are not 'manly'. Nick Watts, a trustee of Men Get Eating Disorders Too, describes an experience of one of their website users – an anorexia sufferer – whose GP's advice to him was simply to 'man up'. It is difficult to imagine that the GP in question would have given a female patient a similarly flippant response.

Eating disorders are also synonymous with depression – a condition which, again, has a tendency to be perceived as something only women suffer from. Logic is traditionally seen as the remit of men, whereas women are emotional creatures. While this view is a little antiquated, the idea is certainly all-pervading enough to influence our perception of eating disorders. Eating disorders are emotional and they certainly aren't logical, and therefore they are seen as a 'female' condition.

Sam and Nick have been surprised by the average age of an MGEDT website user. When Sam initially set up the website, he had anticipated that most of the users would be in their teens and early twenties. However, the website is popular with middle-aged men as well as younger men, who appreciate the anonymity and security the website provides them. In the next chapter when we look at eating disorders and self-esteem education, we will see that there is an increasing demand and need for body confidence to be discussed within the school environment. Perhaps for this reason, young men are generally more able to discuss food and their bodies in a way that their older counterparts are unable or unwilling to do.

To attempt to identify the extent to which this is the case, I conducted a survey among men of different ages to ascertain their awareness of, and attitude towards, eating disorders. All men surveyed have never suffered from an eating disorder themselves.

When asked if they were aware of eating disorders among men, of those in the 16–19 age bracket only 10 per cent said they were not. This isn't altogether surprising, as it's generally acknowledged that eating disorders are more widely recognized as an illness among both genders by younger people. However, in the 40–49 age bracket, a whopping 45 per cent had no concept of male eating disorders. Interestingly, in the 60–69 age category this decreased once more to 33 per cent. Throughout all the age groups questioned, the average percentage of men who were oblivious to eating disorders within their gender was 21 per cent.

The 16- to 19-year-olds then make a fascinating U-turn, with 100 per cent claiming they did not personally know *any* men with a food or body issue (despite the majority of them being aware of them, in principle). The largest percentage of men who conceded that they were aware of a food or body issue in a male acquaintance belonged to the 50–59 bracket, where it stands at more than half – 60 per cent.

The 60- to 69-year-olds then surprise us by being incredibly sensitive to the influence of the media on men's self-perception. Of this age group, 100 per cent surveyed agreed that the media can have a negative effect on self-esteem in males. Astonishingly, only 60 per cent of teenage boys are of the same opinion. The 30- to 39-year-old men take the opposite view to the older generation on this issue, with 100 per cent of them bafflingly claiming that the media has no effect whatsoever on how men feel about their bodies. Overall, there was an acknowledgement of the media's impact to the tune of 79 per cent.

The 30–39 age bracket appear to feel that it is women, rather than the media, who are putting pressure on them to conform to a traditionally attractive look. More than half of them said that the fact that women devote so much time to their appearance adds an expectation that they should do the same. The 50- to 59-year-olds echo this opinion, with 50 per cent in agreement. All other age groups were less convinced of this, and overwhelmingly voted that women's beauty regimes and body image concerns had no bearing on their own.

Finally, when asked if more should be done to raise awareness of eating disorders generally, all age groups unanimously voted 'yes', with the exception of the 40- to 49-year-olds, a staggering 91 per cent of whom voted 'no'.

What can be learned from this survey? Of course, it is mere conjecture, but it would appear from the results that it is the 30–39 age group who have the biggest difficulty in seeing how eating disorders fit into the landscape of their lives and society more generally. This could, of course, be because this age demographic is unlikely to have children in their teens and who therefore have not experienced this issue vicariously. Perhaps the 40–49 age group felt that enough is being done to raise awareness of eating disorders (an unusual opinion) because of the extent to which they are aware of them in their own home.

It is interesting that the older demographic were less aware of male eating disorders but had more personal experience of them, through acquaintances, whereas the teenage boys surveyed were aware of the issues in theory but claimed not to know anyone suffering directly from them.

Over all, we can see that attitudes towards eating disorders among men are, at best, totally confused. However, they are slowly transforming among the public generally and the male eating disorder is increasingly being recognized.

A huge step forward in raising public awareness of eating disorders in men in Britain occurred in April 2008, when the UK was shocked by the news that ex-Deputy Prime Minister John Prescott had suffered from bulimia nervosa.

The story served to debunk many myths – it proved that eating disorders are not the remit of the young, nor those in aesthetically driven careers. It also demonstrated the extent to which the illness can be kept secret – a man who was in the public eye pretty much every day of his several years in office had been suffering behind closed doors, while the nation remained totally oblivious. (In retrospect, Lord Prescott agrees that his chosen profession and being under such close public scrutiny in fact fuelled his eating disorder.)

Lord Prescott says that he decided to go public with his illness when he discovered he was suffering from diabetes as a result of it. The health implications of his condition shocked him into wanting to raise awareness, with the help of Beat (formerly the Eating Disorders Association). Since doing so he says, 'I have received many letters from men who had similar disorders who had been too embarrassed to speak of it.'

Now fully recovered, Lord Prescott believes that more can and should be done to raise awareness of male eating disorders. His experiences show without doubt that men having the courage to come forward and acknowledge their condition can have a positive impact in encouraging other men to seek the help they need.

In this chapter we will investigate the stories of men who have had eating disorders; we will thereby gain some insight into where their issues began and how they felt during their illness, throughout recovery and after their journey back to health. We will give men their rightful voice in the eating disorder arena.

Sam Thomas

Like many bulimia nervosa sufferers, Sam's condition developed at school, as the result of bullying. An academically bright child, he was initially called a 'swot' and other related names. When, aged 14, his voice began to change earlier than his peers', the bullies changed tack, instead relentlessly drawing attention to his voice, which Sam describes as being 'squeaky' and 'effeminate'. Then came the inevitable jibes about his sexuality. Sam says:

> As the bullying became more violent, I would run from the classroom and hide in the toilet, where I would comfort eat as a way of dealing with the turmoil of it all. Then I found I felt uncomfortably full, so it made sense to me to vomit and, in a sense flush my troubles away.

Sam describes perfectly, here, the way the act of bingeing and purging becomes symbolic and initially works as a catharsis to externalize difficult emotions. His story is typical in that what was initially a daily ritual which then became more frequent as the urge to purge became a compulsion. 'I'd be so stressed and upset by the time I came home that I started to binge and purge there, too', he remembers.

Interestingly, Sam claims it simply 'did not occur to me that I had an eating disorder'. Female sufferers often communicate that they were 'in denial' during these early stages of disordered eating. Perhaps because Sam was male, it seems that there simply wasn't enough information available for him to identify his condition early on. This is reinforced by his 'discovery' that he was bulimic aged 15, which happened 'from reading an agony aunt column in one of my mother's magazines'.

Sam eventually sought help from an emergency doctor, who referred him to a counsellor. While, as mentioned, it is important for families to be active participants in the recovery process, we have also emphasized the importance of a bond of trust being established between therapist and patient. The extent to which this is crucial is emphasized by Sam's experience. He had asked his counsellor not to inform his mother or step-father of his illness. They were informed anyway, which, as Sam had anticipated, caused a huge rift within the family. He says that his mother simply 'did not understand'. He was sent to a placement lodging scheme 25 miles from home, which, he says 'gave me stability'.

What ensued, however, was an incredibly painful time for Sam. He began a relationship with someone six years his senior, which then disintegrated because of the strain his bulimia put on them both. Sam then 'made a very positive step' and got in touch with his biological father, discovering at the same time that he had a step-mother and half-brother. He says, 'I found this quite difficult for the first couple of years.'

With all this emotional turmoil, Sam's bulimia worsened. He 'felt suicidal' at this 'dark' time in his life. Sam moved from place to place, initially back to his father's house and then on to another supportive lodging – again, the constant need to 're-start' life and wipe the slate clean is common in bulimia sufferers. This 'etch-a-sketch' approach to living actually mirrors the act of bingeing and purging.

Eventually, however, bulimia patients must acknowledge that, however many times they change location or direction in life, they can never escape themselves. Recovery begins with the realization that they must face and battle their issues, and so it was with Sam. He says:

I knew I had to get on with my life. I was interested in journalism and stated writing letters to newspapers, which lead to writing columns for magazines, etc. I found writing to be good escapism. I worked with various youth workers, which helped a lot and I kept busy. I enjoyed cooking and began to form a good relationship with food. I also found running and working out to be very therapeutic.

This 'distraction' method has its roots in CBT, but the wider philosophy of rediscovering passions and interests in order to let go of a destructive pattern of behaviour is pure NLP.

Sam is now 26 and his last binge was at age 21. He says:

I feel quite distanced from that time now. I'm very proud of my recovery and know how important it is to maintain it. If I was sick again I'd be throwing my new life away, along with my work [Men Get Eating Disorders Too] and the whole social network I have built, who are like my family.

Steve Blacknell

Steve has suffered from both bulimia and anorexia in the past and has now recovered. A former BBC Breakfast radio host and music journalist (most famous for having interviewed Phil Collins during Live Aid, as he crossed the Atlantic in Concorde), he now continues to work in the music, PR and media industries.

Steve has strong opinions on the plight of the male eating disorder sufferer. As a naturally vivacious and talkative character, he believes his path to recovery, a struggle though it was, was easier than that of a shy or less forthcoming man would have been. Steve, like me, believes that the key to conquering eating disorders lays in communication.

Steve describes himself, at the beginning of his career, as a 'cheery but violent, testicle-grabbing rugby prop forward.' He then says, 'Whatever muscle I had turned into flab when I gave up rugby for LSD in 1972.'

Steve's recollections of himself during this time are a fascinating insight into the differences between the male and female psyche. Whereas a woman might say, 'I used to be terribly fat, but I covered up my self-consciousness by being bubbly,' Steve says, 'I was a funny, cheery, but flabby chappie … I could land a good-looking lass with the best of 'em' (he attributes this to his sense of humour).

It seems that Steve positively embraced his identity as a larger-than-life character, both in the literal and metaphorical sense of the word. Pre-eating disorder, his story reinforces the idea that men are much less preoccupied with their physical appearance than women, and it did not seem that he allowed body insecurities to stop him from enjoying his life or pursuing a relationship. He says, 'One such was ''Jo'', a wafer-thin model type. We had a bit of a grassy romp … then one day she informed me that, although I was a lovely man, I was the fattest bloke she had ever been with.'

The impact of Steve's girlfriend's words was colossal. He describes how his 'world crumbled like a hammered grape.'

In 1975, Steve landed a prestigious job within the record industry. Contrary to popular belief, Steve maintains that it wasn't a drug culture which was the problem at this juncture. 'It was food and drink, entertaining the media … and I could feel the pounds coming on.'

It was during one such social occasion that Steve first made himself sick. He rid himself of food at a social event and then proceeded to consume alcohol to give himself a 'buzz'.

This incident developed into a pattern of starving, binge eating and purging which continued until 1979, when Steve became a 'semi-leading light in the ''plugging'' business and the stakes were higher.' He began to starve himself for days on end, tying himself to his bed at night so he could not eat in his sleep. He also took amphetamines as well as tablets to combat fluid-retention. He remembers:

> *This would usually preface a big event where one had to look Slim Jim. Once that was over I would find myself in a food store buying … enough for a month … eat it and throw up. My body didn't know if it was coming or going.*

In 1981 Steve's best friend died suddenly. The event jolted him into confronting his eating disorder. By this stage it 'hurt to throw up.' In a twist of fate, when you consider that a past girlfriend had 'sown the seeds' of his problem to begin with, it was a subsequent girlfriend (now his wife) who encouraged him to seek the therapy which eventually propelled him towards recovery.

Steve used acupuncture to deal with his grief and he also attributes to this the fact that he began the path to self-acceptance. 'I started to feel better about *me*. The hole in my heart was gradually filled. I felt good … deserving … nice.'

Steve opened up about his issue, telling trusted friends and eventually the world – he cannot extol the virtues of talking enough. 'Other men suffer in silence,' he says. 'I wasn't about to do that. Lucky man!' After recovering, he 'came out' on BBC television in 1982, shocking the country with the revelation that men do, in fact, get eating disorders too.

Steve can recall a few isolated incidents when he has relapsed since then. Once was during that famous Concorde flight at Live Aid. He remembers 'hacks gorging on canapés with pictures of starving bodies in my head. I threw up over Wales in the smallest toilet in the air as Queen came on stage to wow them at Wembley.' That was the last time Steve ever made himself sick.

Now, however, Steve 'never thinks' about forcing himself to vomit – although he does concede that his body image is still a problem for him. He'd like to be thinner, but he has 'learned to be OK and it's in control.'

John Stapleton

In April 2008, to coincide with the breaking news of Lord Prescott's bulimia battle, television and radio presenter John Stapleton revealed he had suffered from anorexia nervosa for 20 years. Before that day he had told no one, but he bravely took the momentous step to confess to millions of viewers on BBC's early evening programme *The One Show*.

John is under no illusions as to the influence of pop culture in formulating his illness in the initial stages. He says: 'Being a teenager in the late 1960s, my iconic heroes were people like Mick Jagger and Paul McCartney. They were good looking, had long hair and were thin. I was never fat at all, but maybe a bit plump.'

John decided to lose weight aged 19, when he cut out chips and beer. Then, two weeks before his 21st birthday, he was 'ditched' by this girlfriend, leaving him feeling emotionally vulnerable. Having moved to London to work in Fleet Street, he redoubled his efforts to slim, believing it would make him more attractive to women.

He adds that he 'was under huge pressure at work. Even in those days it was better to be thin than fat, unless you were fat but had something else going for you, such as being funny or eccentric.'

It was at this stage that John began starving himself for up to two days at a time. Living alone in a flat, he had no one to question his eating patterns and it was relatively easy for him to subsist on very little. He recalls that 'alcohol was very much part of the Fleet Street social scene. Having eaten so little, I got drunk very quickly and I just loved the buzz.'

By the age of 23, John describes himself as 'skeletal' He remembers a holiday to Spain during which he spent the entire time with a tee shirt on, saying 'I wanted to take it off, but my chest looked like a toast rack!'

John's recollections demonstrate the 'never thin enough' phenomenon in anorexics. Anorexics often have awareness of their dramatic weight loss, coupled with the contradictory desire to lose yet more weight. John illustrates the inconsistencies in his thinking at this time:

> *Even though I liked what I saw in the mirror, as my face was thinner and my legs were thin, I felt uncomfortable about my chest. Overall I was pleased with my achievement. That is how I saw it – as an achievement.*

John believes if he had approached his GP for help at that time he would have 'been laughed out of the surgery.' He does remember his parents being concerned about him, at one point wrongly convinced that he was taking drugs. He was never diagnosed as anorexic, and only came to a realization about the nature of his condition later in life.

John credits his recovery to the influence of his wife, Lynn, and the effect that moving in with her and settling into a routine had on him. His journey to wellness was gradual, as he ate regular meals because, 'That's what normal couples do!'

John is still careful about what he eats, and remains concerned about being perceived as 'The fat one' on television and the effect this might have on his reputation. It seems, however, that order and control are an inherent part of John's personality, which he has now learned to exhibit in a healthier way. He says, 'I call it professionalism, though some may call it control. I am a bit of a worrier and tend to analyse things ... that's in my character.'

ADVICE TO CARERS

Jenny Langley was moved to write her bestselling book *Boys get Anorexia Too* after her son developed an exercise-based form of anorexia at 12 years old. She now works closely with Men Get Eating Disorders Too, as well as delivering workshops on male eating disorders.

Jenny believes that the problem in diagnosing eating disorders in men arises from three primary factors:

1. With young men, anorexia often initially manifests itself in an obsession with exercise. Jenny's son said he wanted to be a 'stronger runner and football player' and the underlying desire was initially to bulk up, rather than to slim down. Men with eating disorders still see any form of body fat as the enemy, but it is not as simple as wanting to be as slim as possible, especially not in the early stages.

2. Men do not have periods. Jenny therefore asserts that there is 'nothing obvious for GPs to look out for.'

3. Men are less willing to admit that they might have an issue with food, exercise or their lifestyle.

It is this third element which Jenny, Sam Thomas and other eating disorder charities are working towards combating, by providing 'more awareness, more education and more literature.' Jenny also cites internet chat rooms as a huge source of support, especially for carers of men with eating disorders, who 'find it hard to find moral support from local families.'

Jenny stresses the importance of a real understanding of male eating disorders as the most important tool at the carer's disposal. This chapter and the stories that have been shared have hopefully given you some insight and the beginnings of that understanding. While eating disorders in men manifest themselves slightly differently than they do in women, it is critical that carers understand that they stem from the same root: low self-worth.

Craig, who battled with over-eating during his school years, sums this up when he says:

> *Body image issues can be hugely important, and insecurity and low self-esteem is where all [this] stems from ... You constantly seek the approval of others (in my case, it was females). Yet even when you get the approval of other people, you question it, and you only ever feel happy when you are happy with yourself.*

SUMMARY

Colin, who was once sacked after confessing to his boss during a personal conversation that he was anorexic, strongly feels that, 'Although getting a little more press, eating disorders in men are still very misunderstood and poorly recognized.'

Thanks to projects like Men Get Eating Disorders Too, greater awareness of male eating disorders is becoming a reality. Sam Thomas's ultimate vision for MGEDT is to:

Eradicate totally the stereotypical assumptions made about eating disorders, so that men are able to access the same opportunities for treatment and care as their female counterparts. I also feel my vision goes beyond gender and extends to people of any age, background, ethnicity, religion, sexual orientation, etc. After all, eating disorders are indiscriminate and can affect anyone.

Russell Delderfield, whose PhD centres on the male eating disorder phenomenon, further elaborates on this point when he says:

An eating disorder knows few boundaries; it can make its grip felt regardless of disability, ethnicity, sexuality, class, age, location or profession. I really want to bring men's voices together collectively in the hope that this will strengthen the message of all our stories, with the intention that they will add to the courageous individuals who are lone voices out there already.

Steve Blacknell sums up the situation beautifully, with his trademark wit:

Men by definition are a tarty breed, not given to opening up … more likely to talk about West Ham than one's waist measurement. So, on the basis that it's tough enough for this wretched species to communicate on touchy topics such as this, imagine a shy man with a problem.

I am a born communicator. Some are, some aren't. Luckily I have the talent to impart feelings, emotions fears and tears. Others are not so blessed.

Steve is equally vocal in his conviction that men opening up about eating disorders is paramount, not only for the individual concerned, but for progress to be made in this arena more generally: 'If you can, talk about it … People won't think too bad of you … Men, *don't* suffer in silence. Be proud of who you are and just know that there is help out there.'

After all, he says, 'It's a people disease, not a woman's disease.'

CHAPTER 9

EATING DISORDERS AND EDUCATION

When Samantha became very poorly, my first instinct, as a mother, was to take her out of school completely. Her frail state, both mentally and physically, meant that, logically, she wasn't fit for much besides lying on the sofa at home.

There are probably many medical professionals who would argue that this instinct was correct. Physically, certainly, Samantha should have been pretty much sedentary and conserving calories. But, as we now know, eating disorders are a mental illness, and I couldn't help but be concerned as to what keeping Samantha away from the routine of a normal life would do for her mind-set.

As much as I wanted to keep my baby at home and wrap her in cotton wool, I also recognized that this wouldn't be the best way to help her towards recovery. At home she'd have more time to obsess and to focus on food, to navel-gaze and to be gripped further by her demons. Doing nothing day after day would have made her forget who she was. She would have become her eating disorder; it would have defined her and that is an almost insurmountable obstacle to overcome. Once a sufferer allows themselves to believe that their eating disorder is an integral part of them, they'll find it even harder to relinquish it completely.

Looking back, Sam recognizes that our decision to keep her in school was the right one. She also, having learned about the experiences of other ex-sufferers, believes that being placed in full-time medical care might have taught her habits that would have made it even harder for her to get better. Remembering her time in school, she says:

> *Although my exercise and food intake was monitored to an extent whilst I was at school, I still felt a lot freer than I would have done if I hadn't been there. I also now realize how much the teachers supported me and how much extra help they gave me. This helped me to keep up with my studies, which led to me doing really well in my GCSEs – something I never thought I would have been capable of!*

A key part of recovery is allowing a sufferer to see who they are and what their life could be like outside their illness. And so we took the decision that Sam should remain in school and maintain as normal a routine as was possible. This was no easy feat. The decision involved my attending regular, intense and lengthy meetings two or three times a week at the school, and her teachers monitoring her closely, yet in a way which didn't make her feel stifled. I was lucky to have the unequivocal support of the staff at Hinchley Wood Secondary School, Surrey, which allowed us to present a united and consistent front, enabling us to bring Sam back to health.

One particular tricky issue was to negotiate Samantha's love of sport. While, as Sam's disorder developed she had become increasingly obsessed with exercise, attending after-school and evening clubs almost every night, sport had been something she enjoyed before she became ill. Sport was a part of Sam's personality, something which she had to learn to enjoy in a healthy way again during her journey to rediscovering herself.

Luckily, Sam's PE teachers, Leanne and Caroline, recognized this. Caroline says:

> *As a PE teacher you are in a position where you are one of the most likely people in school to spot [an eating disorder]. I think exercise was part of Sam's anorexia, which was why it was so important to keep the fun and social element of it, too, so it didn't just become a bad thing.*

Leanne continues:

> *I kept a close eye on Sam. I let her join in [games] as usual, having made sure she had eaten prior to the lesson (or after-school clubs) because I wanted her to continue to do the things she enjoyed, but not overdo it.*

Samantha also had to eat regularly during the day as she recovered, and her teachers allowed her to eat in class rather than disrupting her routine and embarrassing her by making her leave the lessons to eat at the appointed times. We worked very closely with Melissa, Samantha's form tutor, who was keen to support not only Sam but her sister Charlotte during the challenging months of Samantha's recovery.

Supporting Charlotte was also a pressing concern for us. We were acutely aware that Sam's disorder would affect Charlotte, and that she would at times feel neglected, concerned, resentful, stressed, etc. The school kept an eye on Charlotte and were always sympathetic towards her situation, not just Sam's.

Charlotte, as a protective older sibling (if only by an hour and 20 minutes) felt a huge pressure to look after Sam, and had difficulty in dealing with the stress and worry associated with this responsibility. She became angry and frustrated for a time. She says:

> I felt quite alone and never talked about any of this to anyone, I felt like I had to be the strong one for everyone, especially at school. I had to protect Sammie as we were not at home for Mum or Dad to look out for her. I felt like I was the one who had to be watching all the time. The teachers supported Sammie a lot, and I am so grateful for this. We had a good group of friends around us that were always so patient with us and understanding. However, school years were very difficult and I became someone, looking back on it now, that was totally not me.

A lot of the time, what siblings of sufferers require is simply an acknowledgement that the situation is difficult for them, too. My husband and I were careful to spend time alone with Charlotte and to give her as much attention as we were able to. In retrospect, it was also important that Charlotte felt part of the team giving support and care to Samantha. To exclude her (perhaps misguidedly believing we were protecting her) would have exacerbated the situation.

With regard to Sam, aside from the obvious weight loss, Melissa said she noticed that 'Sam became quite tired, sometimes irritable, pale and withdrawn, especially from her own group of friends.' This initially alerted her to the issue because, as all Sam's teachers were keen to point out, some teenagers lose weight naturally, during the normal course of growing up. Melissa continues:

> *Communication, I believe, was our greatest strength, in conjunction with a mutual desire to help Sammie to recover … Through a mixture of parental instinct, gaining qualifications, and sheer dedication, Lynn has made such a difference to Sam's recovery … Not every girl or boy has access to the support or indeed the education about eating disorders.*

Steven Poole, Samantha and Charlotte's head teacher at Hinchley Wood, points out that, 'This generation are far more aware of food, and far better educated about it, which can make the situation [with regard to eating disorders/body confidence] worse.' Anna, another teacher at the school, adds: 'I think it's more the body confidence issues that should be addressed rather than healthy food.'

Melissa reinforces this idea when she says, of education generally, 'Many PSHE lessons are dedicated to this topic [healthy eating], but can seem to focus on the consequences rather than the potential causes.' Vicky Crocker, who teaches health and social care at Chaucer Technology School in Canterbury, Kent, is very vocal about the necessity for schools to promote personal as well as intellectual development:

When considering self-image and self-concept in young people, it is vital to explore the role of educational establishments and the staff within them. Young people spend much of their time at school and, by very definition, education aims to develop the mind and provide opportunities for personal development.

It is for this very reason that I took the decision to donate a portion of the proceeds of this book to Gossip School, the Body Gossip education programme. (Body Gossip will be discussed further on in this book.) Gossip School sends speakers into schools and colleges throughout the UK to present an hour-long class which addresses self-esteem and body confidence. After the lesson, which encourages students to question their negative beliefs, to have more respect for themselves and for others and to seek any help they might need for a body confidence issue, the teachers within the school or college can follow up with appropriate pastoral care.

Part of the Gossip School lesson does address eating disorders. While not every student in the class will, statistically, suffer from an eating disorder themselves, I believe it is important for every young person to have an understanding of these illnesses. Samantha's best friend, Zoe, echoes this when she recalls their time at school together:

Anorexia. *It was such an outrageous word. It was used as an insult, a compliment or in no context at all. It was misunderstood by so many teenagers, teachers and doctors. It's something so unique to the person that it's incomprehensible to anyone else.*

With eating disorders rising meteorically among the under-25s, it's important for all young people to be aware of them, to provide a network of support for current sufferers and to look out for the signs and symptoms among their peers. They also need to be aware of the dangers and consequences to their health and happiness, in a climate in which eating disorders are often glamorized or glossed over. It is, however, important that this is done in the right way, with an appropriate degree of sensitivity and within a wider context which all students can relate to.

At present some schools have the resources to bring in outside speakers for Personal Social Health & Economic Education (PSHE), while others have to rely on their individual form tutors, which, as Leanne points out, 'can be either good or bad, depending on the tutor's own views and experience.'

Since learning of the wonderful work Gossip School are doing, I wanted to ensure that schools that simply do not have the budget to invite outside speakers to teach body confidence are able to do so, which is exactly what some of the proceeds from this book will do.

Founder of Gossip School Natasha Devon emphasizes the importance of addressing causes rather than symptoms:

When you're working with a room full of 15-year-olds, for example, you're negotiating that precarious line between making them aware of the dangers of eating disorders (and other symptoms of low self-esteem) and just plain giving them ideas. That's why Gossip School is concerned primarily with self-esteem – not only is it getting to the root of the issue, but it's something that every single person in the classroom can relate to.

Natasha, who suffered from an eating disorder herself, first developed Gossip School in 2008 with the idea that she wanted to identify and help other young people with eating disorders. However, after delivering a series of workshops in her local area, she discovered that, not only was body confidence, more generally, a huge issue, but that the consequences of low self-esteem were less distinct or clear-cut. She remembers:

I was shocked to discover that about 99 per cent of the young people had some sort of self-esteem issue in the few schools I visited, and for about 80 per cent of them that manifested itself in something to do with body confidence. When you feel bad about yourself, the easiest thing to do is to direct that discontent at your body. It's real, it's tangible and we're consistently told that it isn't good enough. The aim of Gossip School then became to help students with confidence.

Statistics back up Gossip School's findings. A recent survey revealed that 30 per cent of young men and 70 per cent of young women aged between 11 and 19 cite their relationship with their body as their 'number one worry'. Some 51 per cent of girls are also said to take dangerous risks with their health in pursuit of an impossible beauty aesthetic, with boys following closely behind, at one in five. In any classroom, one in 10 of the students will develop an eating disorder and one in five will be self-harming. Depression, alcohol and drug abuse are also issues schools battle with. All of these issues have their root in low self-esteem.

In Chapter 3 we briefly touched upon 'wannarexia', which, while not technically an eating disorder in the medical sense, is a dangerous condition increasingly affecting teenagers. Many young women are surviving on very little food for days on end in a quest to emulate a super-slender beauty ideal, and young men are being tempted into making dangerous forays into steroids and creatine (a 'nutrition' shake laden with chemicals) to achieve the elusive 'six pack'. It would be futile to quibble about where the line is drawn between an eating disorder and a confused attitude towards food, when the salient fact is that a large proportion of the under-25s are taking dangerous risks with their diet and exercise regimes which could have a severely negative impact on their long-term health.

This is precisely why the common thread of low self-esteem which unites all of these behaviours needs to be emphasized and addressed.

Low body confidence can also easily seep into other areas of the lives of young people. Natasha Devon recalls a teenage girl who approached her after class to ask her about a problem she was having with a fellow student she was dating. This young woman had, correctly as it transpired, made the connection between her sense of self-worth/feelings about her body and her romantic life. Similarly, lack of body confidence can dominate students' minds to such a degree that it affects other areas of their education and, ultimately, their grades. Including classes on self-esteem within the school curriculum, therefore, establishes a strong foundation of confidence upon which young people can build their lives.

While Natasha does share her own eating disorder story during her own workshop, that's purely because, 'Teenagers listen to you when they know you're speaking from personal experience. They don't like being told what to do, especially when it's hypothetical.' The crucial part of the Gossip School workshop is ensuring that the speaker's own story can be made relevant to everyone in the room. This is accomplished by attributing the speaker's own struggles to the power of negative belief, and encouraging students to question their own negative beliefs.

Gossip School then takes the students through a series of exercises which demonstrate how we think, how we perceive the world and are perceived, how everyone thinks differently and how, ultimately, positive belief can effect change for the better in all areas of the students' lives. Natasha is quick to emphasize the crucial differences between awareness-raising and education:

There is little doubt that a graphic, personal story of an eating disorder, or drug addiction, for example, is a powerful tool, but it's not the only tool. I am very concerned with Gossip School presentations not being depressing. Your story is only worth something if you can extrapolate a 'life truth' from it, in terms of education at least. It's also important that the Gossip School presentations, whilst dealing with 'heavy' subject matter, are entertaining. Even at times funny. The aim is not to leave the students feeling depressed!

Samantha, of course, is in a position to comment on this from the perspective of having been a student with an eating disorder, and she agrees with Natasha. Sam says:

> *I feel not all the focus should solely be on food and what you can't do, it should be on what you can achieve and what else you can live for, i.e. friends, hobbies and talents. This I feel will help the sufferer see outside their illness and encourage them to see what they can get better for … it certainly worked for me!*

The biggest surprise for Natasha was when teachers reported that Gossip School was reducing bullying within the schools she visited. She says, 'In retrospect, it makes total sense. We're teaching young people to have more respect for themselves, which in turn means that they have more respect for each other. It's an unexpected, and very welcome, bonus.'

Finally, the workshop addresses the media and advertising, helping students to recognize when they are pursuing an impossible beauty ideal or lifestyle. Natasha, who has personally worked with around 3,000 teenagers between the ages of 13 and 18, since 2008, is anxious that the relationship between young people and the media is not over-simplified. She argues strongly, in her capacity as a body confidence campaigner, that there are myriad sociological factors which lead to children and teenagers wanting to emulate models and pop stars (and perhaps therefore develop 'wannarexia'), and that students are more aware than we might think of the issues at hand. She says:

A lot of the students I work with believe that, if they are not academically bright, they won't get a job – that it's effectively the end of their lives. This isn't because of bad teaching – the vast majority of the teachers I work with are incredibly compassionate and hard-working. It's the education system itself which is fundamentally flawed. We don't accept that each person has a different skill set, that there's more than one way to be clever or talented, and we don't give vocational qualifications any respect.

Vicky Crocker concurs with this point when she attributes the rise in mental health issues among young people, in part, to 'the ever-increasing demands on them to achieve in all subjects, or constantly ... being compared to an average or norm.' Add to that the fact that many teenagers unfortunately do not have a stable home life, and it's little wonder many of them struggle with low self-worth.

Natasha asserts that it isn't, therefore, a belief that models, footballers and pop stars are the pinnacle of achievement that motivates the people who try to emulate them, but the belief that it's the shortcut to everything they feel is outside of their present grasp. Money, acceptance, popularity, success – these are things which many young people feel are impossible in their present lives, and so they covet the life of their favourite celebrity. They see the first step towards that lifestyle as emulating the celeb-esque body. It's the one thing young people feel they can control, when so many areas of their lives seem out of control, or utterly devoid of hope.

As a parent, this is something worth knowing. Often parents try to counteract extreme diets or a sudden gym obsession by telling their children that they are 'fine' or 'gorgeous' just the way they are. Having had an insight into many teenagers' motivations for embarking on extreme dietary and exercise regimes, it appears that this well-meaning gesture might not always be the correct tactic.

We must remember, in this instance as with all eating-disordered behaviour, that we are dealing with symptoms rather than causes. It's far more effective to think around the issue – is your child having a difficult time at school or within their friendship groups? Focus on their emotional wellbeing rather than on treating the issue as a looks-based one.

Gossip School, as an organization, base their work on the idea that the solution to lack of body confidence lays in changing individual mind-sets, rather than wrestling with the Goliath that is the media. Natasha says:

> *Confidence is like a suit of armour, and if there is a chink in that armour then the more negative aspects of the media or advertising can sneak in and plant seeds of doubt. But if the suit is strong and impenetrable, outside influences cease to be an issue. By encouraging students to recognize their unique talents and celebrate their individuality, we help them to build their armour.*

We will explore the contentious issue of the role of the media in creating or fuelling eating disorders in Chapter 14.

In reality, sadly, there is no shortcut to combating the low-self-worth epidemic in young people. The answer lies in allowing teenagers to understand their value and recognize their talents, and in so doing allowing them to see that they can be successful without becoming a carbon copy of someone else. Natasha echoes this sentiment: 'We like to think we help students to be the best version than themselves, rather than a rubbish version of someone else!'

Body Gossip works in conjunction with a number of charities and groups, so that Gossip School can refer students to appropriate sources of information and support, if necessary. Natasha says:

> *There's a difference between giving someone the benefit of your experience, or teaching them, and giving them advice. Advice is where teachers, who have been incredibly supportive, or the student's parents, or outside organizations would step in. We all work together to provide a network of support, and that's incredibly important.*

Insecurity is, to a certain degree, a normal part of growing up. However, self-esteem education programmes such as Gossip School are not only helping students address the issues that they might be facing in the present, it's also arming them with the knowledge they need to tackle future problems. In short, it's an investment in the future of our children.

SUMMARY

Throughout this book I have been careful to emphasize that eating disorders do not affect just the young. However, sometimes the underlying issues can begin to develop and form at this crucial age. The teenage years can be difficult for anyone, as identities and the world are explored and boundaries are pushed. It is a time when, arguably, we are at our most insecure and uncertain.

Schools, colleges and, in particular, universities are an environment where eating disorders can flourish. Outside the routine of the home and the supervision of parents or guardians, not to mention amid peer pressure, eating disorders have found a chink in the armour of otherwise coherent and healthy guidance. Self-esteem education is therefore an essential ally for carers, and indeed, all parents.

Money in schools is notoriously tight and what are considered 'fluffy' subjects are usually the first to get cut. I'd encourage all schools to recognize that this can be short-sighted. As Natasha says, 'All the qualifications in the world are no substitute for being content in your own skin.'

Vicky Crocker summarizes the situation when she says:

I hope in time all schools across the UK will invest the time and money needed to face this problem head-on to ensure that these figures peak and begin to decrease. Further education is needed to reduce the stigma attached to

emotional and mental health problems. Young people face
many pressures, and, in an ever-changing society, we must do
all we can to support them in becoming happy and confident
adults.

As Natasha and Vicky have illustrated, where schools can, they
should incorporate self-esteem into their programme – and
preferably from an outside speaker. I say this not because I
believe teachers are ill-equipped to deal with the issues, but
because I know that young people will often open up to a
stranger, safe in the knowledge that they will never see that
person again. Prevention is better than cure, of course, and
I firmly believe self-esteem education can help to stop body
confidence issues in their early stages. If an eating disorder
has developed, however, schools can provide a more intensive
role, as was the case with Samantha's school, Hinchley Wood.
Without their support it would not have been possible for her
continue a relatively normal routine, which has been essential to
her recovery. Communication was our most important and most
powerful tool, allowing myself, Samantha's teachers, Charlotte
and their peer group to work together in supporting her towards
recovery.

It is essential that everyone involved in the life of a sufferer
employs compassion, understanding and patience. In this way,
schools can become an effective part of the caring network for
young people struggling with eating disorders.

CHAPTER 10

EATING DISORDERS AND SPORT

When considering the role sport plays in eating disorders, it is important to realize that there are two distinct perspectives. We have briefly touched upon the fact that anorexics and bulimics often exercise compulsively. We will explore this a little more during this chapter, and also look at how a healthy balance can be achieved, during and after recovery. However, it is also important to acknowledge that eating disorders are rife within the professional sporting world.

When we think of an industry in which eating disorders are likely to flourish, it is common to cite fashion or beauty. However, the intensely competitive nature of sport, coupled with the unspoken (or occasionally, verbalized) rule that the lower the contestant's weight, the more they will excel in their field, means that it is also common to see eating disorders within professional sports. Jockeys, dancers and gymnasts are statistically particularly at risk, as well as body-builders. Indeed, any sport in which the focus is on aesthetics and artistry, as well as performance, is an environment in which an eating disorder can thrive. Lori Henry, a former dancer who has now recovered from bulimia nervosa, says:

> *I believed having a sculpted body would help me in dance class, where I stared at my thighs in the mirror four days per week, seeing them as flabby extensions of my fleshy stomach, when in reality I had an average-sized body for my 5 ft 2 frame.*

This is not to suggest that all professional sportspeople have disordered eating habits. Indeed, unusual eating patterns, for example consuming high levels of lean protein, are necessary to a degree within some sports. However, as a carer it is important to be vigilant against potentially risky environments and behaviours.

Later in this chapter, two professional sportspeople who have suffered from eating disorders will share their experiences, as well as a mother and daughter who were very involved in gymnastics, and a man who used athletics as part of his recovery from anorexia. They will provide us with an insight into the sporting world and the pressures faced by athletes, both on an amateur and a professional level. However, first let's examine a little more closely the role which exercise plays within eating disorders.

Exercise provides the same basic conundrum as food: if a person becomes addicted to it, it is not possible to give it up altogether. Moderate physical activity is essential for optimum health. Therefore, the challenge for anorexics or bulimics in recovery is to strike a healthy balance of exercise within their lifestyle, without allowing themselves to become obsessed. Equally, learning to enjoy exercise can play a fundamental role within recovery. Wendy Martin, a lecturer in sports and sports therapy, says:

> *Exercise is essential if we are to lead a healthy and fulfilling life. The physical benefits have been widely reported for many years ... Psychological benefits should not be neglected and can play an extremely powerful role in the road to recovery for many individuals who have experienced disorders of the mind. Chemical activity triggered by exercise can reduce anxiety, stress and depression and can also play a role in improving immune function.*

The message, here, is that sport and exercise are not the enemy, contrary to the beliefs of many. In order to gain some clarity with regard to how to navigate the precarious line between beneficial and compulsive exercise, I commissioned a survey of more than 500 past and present sufferers, with a view to finding out what approach they take to exercise.

All participants in the survey were over the age of 16. Around 75 per cent were female. Of those surveyed, 38.1 per cent said they participated in strenuous exercise more than three times per week (for example, going to the gym). It is important to note that this is not recommended by medical professionals, who state that three times a week is the optimum number of times to perform strenuous exercise for people who are not training for a specific event. The most popular reason cited for undertaking this exercise was to maintain a desired body shape/look good. Having said that, almost half of those surveyed said they wanted to maintain a 'healthy body and mind', although 30.3 per cent also said they wanted to lose weight. From these statistics it is clear that some unhealthy attitudes and behaviours have lingered within the participants' minds.

At the conclusion of the survey, participants were asked if they had anything to add which they felt was important. Bearing in mind that we do not know the nature of the participants' past or present body or eating issues, below are some of the more interesting and positive replies, which demonstrate how to achieve a healthy balance:

- I do yoga class once a week and yoga at home three times per week. I walk 40 minutes daily, quite fast, and walk on escalators. I go out dancing about once a month. Basically, I move for fun and/or to get me somewhere!

- I don't do as much intense exercise as I would like, but I have previously been in a place where I became obsessive, so the gym is not a good environment for me. I've found a balance by walking everywhere, up to five miles every day, which allows me to stay toned and really clears my head.

- I exercise because I enjoy it. I enjoy training for an outcome, whether to relieve stress or make the squad. I need to have some motivation, whether it's someone running by my side or something to aim for.

- It is important to relax properly after exercise so I meditate and/or pause and that gives me a more balanced perspective on life.

- Exercise, combined with sensible eating, enables me to stop stressing as much about my weight and body shape.

- I find exercise extremely empowering. Many believe that it is negative for people who are recovering from an eating disorder to take part in exercise, however I have found weight training and sports supplements vital in my weight gain and in my recovery.

What we learn from these comments is that it is possible to find an exercise regime that complements recovery and a healthy, balanced lifestyle, but it is important to examine the motivations behind exercise in order to do so. The most important factors are:

- The sufferer, or past sufferer, should choose a form of exercise they enjoy. Exercise should never seem like a punishment.

- The sufferer or past sufferer should steer clear of any environments in which they once exercised compulsively, or used exercise to purge, prior to their decision to recover.

- The motivation for exercise should always be to maintain a healthy mind and body – that might mean losing weight for compulsive or binge eaters, but that is a side-effect rather than the main goal.

As a carer your role might be to introduce your loved one to a form of sport or exercise they haven't tried before and which is fun and not too strenuous. Dance classes are always a good option in this regard, as is swimming. It's also crucial for recovering anorexics and bulimics to acknowledge that if they are exercising more, they will need to increase their calorie intake to allow their body to cope with the demands of physical activity. The following testament, from one of the participants of my survey, along with my own experiences with Samantha, mean that I do not believe banning exercise altogether is effective:

> *I have been on an exercise ban for 1.5 years and it still kills me every day. Everyone is so obsessed with exercise and calories, even people without eating disorders. My recovery has been so slow – I exercise in secret to stop from gain[ing] weight and to make me feel less guilty for going against the grain and having to eat more.*

In this instance, the recovering anorexic has been told, metaphorically, 'not to think of a pink elephant'. If she were allowed to exercise publicly in moderation and to enjoy it, then rather than see it as necessary in order to burn calories, it might very well do wonders for her mind-set.

Conversely, in Sam's case she was allowed to exercise moderately, with guidelines set by myself and her school, during her recovery. Sport had been a large part of Samantha's life prior to her becoming ill and, as I have emphasized regularly throughout this book, it is essential that sufferers are allowed to glimpse what their life might be like when they recover, to give them something to hope for. We therefore compromised with Samantha, allowing her to participate in sport as long as she agreed to up her calorie intake to compensate. There were additional benefits, in that sports gave Sam a sense of normality, allowing her to socialize, which in turn prevented her from feeling isolated. She says:

Mum and my school still allowed me to train and run in races, which I had loved before I became poorly. Obviously I wasn't exercising as much as I had before and I also had to be monitored very closely. However, I feel this was the right decision and [it] did really help with my recovery, as it kept me focused and meant I was still socializing with my friends.

It's also important to consider, at this stage, that gyms have their own role to play in identifying compulsive exercisers. Of course it is not solely the responsibility of the gym to spot and prevent eating disorders, however most good gyms have a policy whereby they will intervene if they believe someone is over-exercising or losing an excessive amount of weight.

In Chapter 7 we saw that Professor Janet Treasure's research has revealed that there are certain personality types statistically more likely to suffer from eating disorders. This does not mean that eating disorders are inevitable for these people, simply that they are a little more at risk. One personality trait which crops up frequently is a super-competitive nature. People who feel they constantly need to strive to be better in order to be accepted often use the skill of pushing themselves to succeed in order to lose weight. Professional and amateur athletes are, by their very nature, always striving to better their performance, which immediately puts them into Professor Treasure's 'at risk' category even before they have experienced the demands and pressures of the industry. Wendy Martin elaborates: 'It is evident that those that take part in sport face numerous pressures and, combined with the typical society pressures individuals face to achieve a certain body type, it is not surprising that athletes often succumb to these pressures.'

Below are the stories from the sporting world which will help us shine a light on the eating issues which often arise from it.

Suzanne Dando

Suzanne is a former Olympic gymnast and British gymnastic champion. Having competed at a world level within her sport since the age of 12, Suzanne suffered a sports injury five years later, to which she attributes her subsequent spiral into anorexia. She says, 'At the vulnerable age of 17, recovering from a sports injury and conscious of not wanting to put on weight, I cut down considerably on my food intake ... I lost my strength, muscle tone, determination and self-worth.'

Suzanne did not seek professional help for her condition, but instead relied on her parents and coaches for support and guidance, which she describes as 'the best therapy for my situation' (thereby reinforcing just how crucial carers are!).

The key element of Suzanne's recovery was the 'gentle persuasion' the people around her used to enable her to see that, by not fuelling her body, she was throwing away all the hard work she had put into becoming a world-class sportsperson. They would remind her that her goal was to become the country's top gymnast and that she would not achieve this unless she allowed herself to eat. Suzanne says:

> *I wanted to get better because I didn't want to fail. I have always believed that it was the love of my sport and my own stubborn determination to win that got me over those first difficult hurdles ... My reward a couple of months later was to be allowed back into training.*

What is so inspiring about Suzanne's story is that the exact same traits which initially fuelled her eating disorder were also the ones which allowed her to get better. This is something I often tell my clients: It takes willpower and single-mindedness and a certain amount of strength to starve oneself, and these are the exact same attributes which can be focused towards recovery to propel the sufferer towards a happy and healthy life.

Ian Sockett

Suzanne Dando's belief that sport and the sportsperson's mind-set can be used in a positive way during recovery is further reinforced by the example of Ian Sockett.

Ian suffered from anorexia nervosa for some 20 years. He is now an ambassador for Men Get Eating Disorders Too and regularly speaks at events, in which he shares his experiences.

Ian had always harboured a desire to run a marathon, but his illness had prevented this from becoming a reality. As he recovered, he focused on his ambition to train for a marathon and the food became a necessary fuel for his body so that he could achieve that dream. He says, 'finishing that 26.2-mile race became my goal and food now became my friend.'

Ian harnessed the huge amount of willpower and determination he had used in order to starve himself, and channelled it into training. Whenever he felt a temptation to relapse he would remember the charities who were depending on him to complete the race, and this would spur him on. Sport also helped Ian to rediscover his sense of self (a fundamental part of eating disorder recovery). He says:

> *The marathon was bigger than the anorexia ... 4th April 2009 I crossed the line of the Paris marathon in 4 hours and 4 minutes. I was alive. I was bursting with pride and self-belief. I embraced my parents and we sobbed with happiness.*

Martina Eberl Ellis
Martina is a professional golfer and a familiar face on the golfing circuits of Europe since turning professional in 2002.

Martina's dysfunctional relationship with food began around the age of 12, although she did not acknowledge that she had an eating disorder until she was 15. At this stage she was using sport as a way of purging, after gorging on a 'huge amount of sweets every day'. She also began to use laxatives.

Martina attributes her sickness to 'wanting to be perfect'. She describes herself as 'longing for attention, for success'. The desire for perfection didn't just apply to Martina's sporting life, but leaked into every aspect of her existence. No one is perfect in every way, and yet the constant feelings of disappointment Martina experienced drove her to depression and to bulimia. Now recovered, Martina understands that 'failing is perfectly normal and you should just try to be the best that you can be.'

When reflecting on the role her environment played in her illness, Martina says:

> I think there is pressure in the sporting world for women to conform to a certain look. The media is brutal. They take the worst pictures and make them even worse, just to make fun of you … You can also tell by signing contracts with sponsors. The better-looking girls get more of them and make more money, although they might not play better.

In a later chapter we will explore the influence of the media in creating and fuelling eating disorders. Martina is quick to point out that, as far as female sportspeople are concerned, we should bear in mind that it is 'about sport, not modelling.'

Martina's story teaches us that danger can arise when the compulsion to be exceptional (which motivates many sportspeople to excel in their field) bleeds into other areas of their lives. As a carer it is therefore important to emphasize to your loved one that, while their competitive nature is a bonus when they are competing, they are loved and accepted for who they are, 'flaws' and all.

Louise and Doreen

Louise, an amateur gymnast, joined a gym club which encouraged her to lose weight in order to be 'healthy'. This heralded an unhealthy obsession with weight loss. She remembers: 'When I was at the gym it was drilled into us that to put on weight was a failing and we were judged and criticized for this.'

Her mother adds:

> *Enormous pressure was put on the gymnasts to lose weight. They were weighed both before and after training. They were given target weights to attain, which were in some cases unrealistic. They were often lined up and certain gymnasts were then told to go and run around the field several times because they needed to lose weight. Ridicule and humiliation was also used.*

Louise has still not overcome her eating disorder entirely. However, she has acknowledged her problem and is trying various methods of therapy in order to conquer it. She practises yoga, and says that she finds this gentle and soothing form of exercise helpful.

Louise's mother believes that the solution lies in greater awareness-raising of eating disorders within gymnastics (specifically), as well as a change in how gymnastic clubs are run and supervised.

SUMMARY

Throughout the examples used in this chapter we have seen the importance of moderation and balance when it comes to sport and exercise.

Parents, coaches and gym staff should be vigilant to the early signs of obsession with physical exercise. However, it is important to remember as a carer that if your loved one is very sporty then the drive and determination they employ in practising their sport can be turned into positive and crucial aspects of their recovery.

CHAPTER 11

EATING DISORDERS AND ETHNICITY

Our cultural programming is so all-pervading and thoroughly embedded that we might not even be aware of the extent to which it influences us. For many young women, for example, it begins as early as the moment when they watch their first feature-length cartoon featuring a doe-eyed, super-slender heroine being rescued by a brave and handsome prince. Somewhere in the subconscious, a belief begins to form – a belief that women should be skinny and helpless and that it is the men in their lives who will determine their destinies. Young men are equally susceptible, constantly aware of the need to live up to the 'tall, dark and handsome' ideal.

Outmoded ideals stretching as far back as the Victorian age still remain prevalent in our society. Many feminist writers and thinkers believe anorexia in women arises, in part, out of a belief that sufferers do not think that they deserve to take up space (and should therefore shrink until they become invisible).

The effect of the media in the body-image debate is something which is endlessly dissected and discussed and, indeed, there is a chapter devoted to it later on in this book. However, it would be remiss to suggest that there is one central and unified culture which influences us. Britain and the United States, in particular, pride themselves on being diverse, multi-cultural countries. If you perhaps work in a school, or are part of the medical community, it is important to understand the wide-ranging cultural elements which might be influencing a sufferer's thought processes.

To give us an insight into how different ethnicities and cultures might feel about their bodies, I have asked four women from four different cultural backgrounds (but resident within the UK) to share their feelings about their bodies and food. I've also invited them to share any thoughts or opinions they have about their ethnic background and how it has influenced them and other people within it.

It is important to note, at this point, that this is by no means an exhaustive list. This chapter includes case studies from a broad range of ethnic backgrounds, however, again, each individual is unique. The focus of this section of the book is to demonstrate how cultural influences can play a part in the eating-disordered mind-set. It's important to acknowledge, though, that this will happen to a lesser or a greater extent in each individual – especially when you bear in mind the rapidly increasing number of mixed race people in our society who are the product of two or more cultures, each with its own blend of influences.

Jacqui

Jacqui is 47 years old and of Chinese heritage, born and brought up in the UK. Her husband is Singaporean and she visits Singapore frequently to see family. At 5 ft 6 and a size 12 (US size 8), Jacqui feels she is healthy and slim within the context of the UK norms. However, when she travels to Singapore she becomes acutely aware of the discrepancies in culture, and believes that they might be potentially dangerous, even promoting anorexia. She says:

> *Singapore is a multi-cultural society, most admirable as its different cultural and religious groups live relatively harmoniously together. The obsession with being slim does not seem to be religious in any way. It is a pressure brought on by society and the media, like the West but more so, I feel.*
>
> *The women in Singapore are genetically smaller and indeed shorter, however what they class as normal is so different.*
>
> *The shops [in Singapore] do not stock what they call 'large sizes' (I am an XXL over there). When I visit a chemist or a health shop the sales assistant actually offers me diet pills, which I haven't asked for.*
>
> *If I went to Singapore to live I feel I would have to lose a considerable number of pounds simply to fit in!*

Jacqui also notes how all-pervading the beauty and fitness industry is in Singapore. The press is inundated with advertisements for slimming clinics. Every shopping centre has 'health and beauty centres galore'. Jacqui visited one such centre and was given a target weight which would have put her in a dangerously low BMI range in the UK.

Jacqui is keen to point out that this situation has not arisen because all Singaporean women 'do not eat'; she simply feels that the lack of diversity and worryingly slender norms might have a detrimental effect on many young people living in the country, if they happen to be naturally a little larger. She worries that her children, who are 18 and 22 years of age, compare themselves to their Singaporean relatives, and says 'it is very hard to reassure them that they look lovely and, indeed, are very slim by Western standards.'

Jasmine

Jasmine is 18 years old. She is Muslim and her family's origins are in the Middle East. She is currently recovering from bulimia nervosa. She has found it hard to open up to her family about her condition or to seek the help she needs, in part owing to religious and cultural pressures.

Born and raised in the UK, Jasmine feels that there is a duality between what is expected of her as a Muslim and the pressure to fit a certain beauty aesthetic which is placed on her by British culture. She says, 'I think Muslim women are supposed to take pride in their appearance, but Islam has taught me that appearance and body image should not define me as a woman, hence the reason I started wearing the hijab.'

In terms of eating disorders, Jasmine believes that 'Muslim women are aware of the issues, they simply don't discuss them.'

Significantly, Jasmine feels that Arab and Middle Eastern beauty paradigms have been heavily influenced by the West in recent years. She says:

Just from watching old Arab films (especially Egyptian), women were big, and that was acceptable. Arab/Muslim women living in the Middle East have been heavily influenced by a Western ideal of beauty since then. Some of my family have become obsessed with Western beauty ideals.

In Muslim families, as in Jewish ones, there is also an emphasis placed on food as a means of being sociable. A recent survey published online reported that Jewish women can be twice as likely as non-Jewish women to suffer from bulimia, because of the expectation placed upon them to consume large quantities of food at family gatherings. However the report also suggested that this is largely unacknowledged. Jasmine says of her own experiences:

For me, one of the major issues is that I couldn't see other Muslim woman I could relate to, in the public eye. The minority sufferers are always ignored, be they Muslim or any other ethnic group. I didn't feel I was normal. I was constantly thinking, 'Am I the only Muslim going through this?'

Esther

Esther is a British woman in her twenties. Her roots are in Nigeria. She is naturally of a slim build and this caused her some discomfort over the years, since Nigerian culture (in sharp contrast to British) holds very curvaceous women up as the ultimate beauty ideal. She says:

I think a lot of West African women over-eat. Traditionally, bigger woman are seen to be richer, wealthier women. Having more weight shows that you have been eating and you are 'well'. As a British woman I am very aware and concerned with staying in shape. That's not really in the mind of African women. What is seen to be 'eating well' in African culture would be seen as over-eating in the UK.

Esther now appreciates and accepts her naturally slender body and has learned not to compare herself to her Nigerian family, but does say that she thinks their 'curves are out of this world!'

Kered

Kered is originally of West Indian descent. She is the editor of online magazine *Complexd*, which features women from a diverse range of ethnic backgrounds and of all shapes and sizes. She believes strongly that *Complexd* magazine's work is helping to combat a potentially damaging beauty norm.

Kered has had the benefit of working with a wide range of varying cultures in her capacity as editor of *Complexd*. Discovering all women have something they feel insecure about. Like Esther, Kered is naturally petite, which is at odds with the prevailing Afro-Caribbean beauty paradigms, but conforms to those within British culture. She says:

When I am visiting family in the Caribbean, the first thing they say (followed by giving me a large plate of food) is, 'Girl, you need fattening up!' Men in the Caribbean worship curvier women, and women with curves are extremely confident with flaunting their figures. I try to maintain a neutral attitude towards my body and its changes.

Kered believes that Afro-Caribbean women might be at less risk of developing anorexia because, culturally, eating, cooking and curves are celebrated. She says that, although she has come to embrace and celebrate her own body, if she 'put on weight I really wouldn't mind.'

SUMMARY

Jacqui, Jasmine, Esther and Kered have all demonstrated that there is not one global beauty ideal, which is heartening to an extent (if only because it means that attitudes are fluid and have the potential to change). They are each aware of the influence their heritage has had on their attitudes towards their respective bodies and how they eat, but equally they are aware of and susceptible to Western beauty ideals.

We have seen that Jewish and Muslim women might be a little more at risk of bulimia, East Asian women could develop anorexia if they are not naturally as slender as their peers, and that Afro-Caribbean women might be more prone to over-eat. However, none of these is by any means a hard and fast rule. An individual's eating habits cannot be gauged solely by their ethnic background. Cultural influences are merely another contributing factor to take into consideration when attempting to comprehend the mind-set of someone with an eating disorder.

CHAPTER 12

EATING DISORDERS AND THE ELDERLY

When we think of older people's attitude towards eating disorders, it conjures up images of a stern and uncomprehending person saying, 'What do mean, she won't eat? We fought a war, you know!' Most of us simply don't include anyone over the age of 40 years of age in our notion of the body-image debate.

This attitude, although understandable, is both overly simplistic and downright inaccurate. Eating disorders have been shown to affect older people in a number of ways, but this demographic are even less likely to be accurately diagnosed than their younger counterparts.

It has been shown, for example, that people who suffer from and conquer an eating disorder in their early lives can sometimes suffer a relapse when they retire. This is because of the sudden change in the pace of their lifestyles and the unsettling and sometimes frightening nature of this change. Eating disorders can be a 'coping mechanism' when life becomes difficult, and so it can be that people revert back to long-forgotten habits at retirement age.

There are also those elderly people who have 'managed' an eating disorder their entire lives. We will see an example of this later on in this chapter. Most often, in these cases, the older person's illness was noticed when they were younger, but because of the lack of understanding in the medical profession, or in society more generally when they first became ill, they were not given the treatment they needed. Then, even more so than now, eating disorders were seen as part of an individual's 'personality'. Add to this the all-pervading myth that eating disorders are a life sentence, and it is little wonder that many elderly sufferers have been put off seeking help.

Then there is the issue of older people's attitudes to talking or mind-based therapies to throw into the mix. While of course in 2012 the idea of having a counsellor or therapist is very normal indeed, this has only been the case for a relatively short period of time. Many older people are unaware of, or unwilling to acknowledge the existence of, mental illnesses such as depression and eating disorders. They might also consider therapy for these conditions self-indulgent and unnecessary.

Finally, there are those older sufferers whose condition has developed later in life. This can occur for a number of reasons – some physical, some practical and some psychological. We will explore some of these reasons below.

While, usually, eating disorders which begin in old age do have slightly different causal factors than those which start when the sufferer is younger, they may manifest themselves in a different way. There can be little doubt that anorexia, in particular, is a huge problem within the retired community. In 1990, the University of British Columbia conducted a study of 10.5 million death certificates in the US, regarding deaths which had occurred over the previous five years. The study found that anorexia strikes more elderly people than had been previously acknowledged by either the medical community or the general public. In fact, the average age of death from anorexia was 69 for women and 80 for men.

As eating disorders among the over-sixties have been increasingly acknowledged, awareness has also been raised of bulimia within that demographic. This was also shown to be a significant issue – although older people were discovered to be more likely to abuse laxatives than to purge by making themselves sick.

As stated above, older people have their own set of challenges which are distinct from those faced by their younger counterparts, but these challenges can still, ultimately, result in an eating disorder. The key, as ever, is to look at an eating disorder as a symptom, rather than a cause, and to consider the causal elements which might have given rise to it.

It may be, of course, that the physical issues older people face naturally give rise to an eating disorder, without a psychological element being present. However, as our interview with Professor Janet Treasure has shared with us, eating disorders ultimately develop in layers and become psychological eventually. For example, as people get older they are likely to experience medical problems, and these problems may make it difficult for them to consume or digest food. They may have difficulty swallowing or chewing, bowel issues, poor digestion or they may be taking medication which leads to a loss of appetite. These will all lead to starvation of the brain.

Dementia has been closely linked to anorexia. The two are self-perpetuating because, as we have seen, the brain must be fed in order to function properly. There is also the possibility that memory loss can lead to sufferers not remembering whether or not they have eaten.

Of course there are also psychological causal reasons behind eating disorders in the elderly and, as with all eating disorders, these are the hardest to address and combat.

Bereavement can be a huge factor in eating disorders in people of all ages. In some instances, people who have developed an eating disorder in their teens strongly identify the first death of a loved one which they had to contend with as the incident which gave rise to their condition. So it is little wonder that the elderly also respond to grief by developing a disordered relationship with food and their bodies. Older people are statistically more likely to lose their spouses, siblings and friends, so this is a particular problem for their age group. Bereavement often, irrationally, leads to feelings of guilt as well, of course, as isolation and loneliness, all of which are emotions familiar to eating disorder sufferers.

Additionally, if an older person finds themselves living alone because of the death of a partner, having been used to cooking for two they will often 'not see the point' of cooking for themselves. This is particularly true of women, who may have seen themselves in the more traditional care-giving role within a family – but have not been used to caring for themselves.

There can be a huge element of attention-seeking when it comes to the elderly and eating disorders. Because of the way older people are usually treated in Western society, they tend to feel as though they are not listened to or acknowledged. Eating disorders are often a cry for help, or a way to alert family members or carers to how they are feeling, without having to go through the indignity of articulating the same. The older generation are known for being quite stoic when it comes to their emotions, so it may well be that they simply don't know how to talk about how they are feeling. Instead, and perhaps without even being consciously aware of it, their inner concerns may be expressed through disordered eating.

Eating disorders are even more deadly for elderly people than for younger sufferers, because the older a person is, the more likely they are to have problems with their physical health. Elderly people are also often alone, meaning that their eating habits are not effectively monitored.

If caring for a younger person with an eating disorder is difficult, caring for your elders is twice as hard. Throughout their lifetimes they have probably established a dynamic whereby they are the care- or advice-giver, and having to reverse this, for whatever reason, is always hard. Older people are also adept at hiding their behaviours and their feelings.

These obstacles to recovery may appear insurmountable for carers. There is undoubtedly more of a stigma attached to eating disorders in the elderly. While we are used to seeing, in the press, sufferers in their teens, twenties and thirties, it is rare to see an eating disorder story featuring someone over the age of 40, or to hear it discussed in social circles. When researching this book I came across many elderly sufferers who were immensely grateful that this issue is being tackled and brought to light, but who were not prepared to share their own stories publicly. There is a huge conspiracy of silence surrounding older people's experience of eating disorders and it's a vicious circle – the less they speak out, the less others are willing to.

It therefore takes a very brave person to admit to their condition. I was delighted when Pat agreed to share her story with the readers of my book and help to raise awareness of an issue which is all too often swept under the carpet.

Pat's Story

Pat is currently 59 years of age and has suffered from anorexia since she was in her late teens. She is an identical twin and, tragically, lost her sister to complications arising from her own eating disorder back in 2004.

Although she is technically a healthy BMI, Pat would not describe herself as 'in recovery'. She says:

Recovery is a lot of things. It's being a healthy weight, but it also has to do with your mental wellbeing. Anorexia is always there, in my mind. I have learned to manage my condition and to maintain my weight at a healthy level, mainly because of the risk of osteoporosis, but I don't feel free of the condition.

Like many people who struggle with eating disorders and are over 40 years of age, Pat believes that the people around her see her illness as a part of her personality and an inevitable 'blight' on her life. She states without any trace of self-pity that 'people have long since lost sympathy' with her, and she does not seem to hold out any hope that she will ever be completely cured. As we have discussed above, this is a common obstacle when attempting to address eating disorders in older patients – many have reconciled themselves to their fate. This is usually in part due to the lack of adequate treatment for eating disorder patients in previous years. Pat believes that, where possible, eating disorders should be nipped in the bud:

If you even think you might have an eating disorder, take a deep breath and go and see your GP. I don't want to scare young people, but at the same time it is so important that eating problems are addressed early.

When Pat first became ill, she says that eating disorders were perceived as a 'very different animal. We didn't have the internet. We didn't have counsellors. We only had our GP. Therapy just wasn't something you did.'

Pat was separated from her twin sister when they both attended university. Neither dealt with the separation well, and she attributes this to the beginning of their eating problems. When they came back from university, they shared a house. Pat recalls that there was a huge competitive element between them. 'We had to eat the same and we had to be the same weight. It is the only thing I can ever remember us competing over.'

Their illness escalated during their twenties, as the two of them unwittingly spurred on each other's condition. When their mother died, Pat and her sister received bereavement counselling which also helped them to tackle their anorexia, to an extent. Because of this, Pat can see the value of counselling and does still go to counselling sessions, though not as frequently as she once did.

Pat regularly visits the Beat online forum for carers, as she herself cared for her twin sister for many years. She manages her issues using alternative therapies and beauty treatments. She says that she 'looks after herself' and that this is key to her feeling good enough to allow her to maintain a healthy weight.

She says, 'I have what I suppose is a ''normal'' life, but I can be prone depression. I've given up hope that I'll ever get better, but I fight tooth and nail every day to keep myself healthy.'

Pat is determined to raise awareness of eating disorders among the over-fifties. She laments the fact that there does not appear to be any specialist help for older sufferers of eating disorders at present, and believes that many older people are 'suffering silently'. She works alongside Beat to look at different ways to address this, and believes that if more medical attention was given to the issue, 'It would save the NHS a heck of a lot, in the long term.'

Pat has bravely spoken out about her illness in the national press, and her story demonstrates how many older people have given up hope of ever recovering. However, it is important to remember that recovery is possible at any age, with the right combination of treatments.

It is crucial to bear in mind that, no matter how old a sufferer may be, their illness is not part of who they are. The sufferer and the people around them must never give up hope.

SUMMARY

Eating disorders are prevalent among the elderly. However, as we have seen throughout this chapter, the causes often differ from those of their younger counterparts. Whether it is physical deterioration, bereavement, loneliness, attention-seeking or having 'managed' and become accustomed to an eating disorder which started earlier in life, there is a solution to eating disorders among older sufferers.

Carers will struggle to convince older sufferers that they should seek help. However, with increased awareness and the public testimony of brave individuals like Pat, the stigma will soon lessen and, eventually, disappear.

It's also important to acknowledge at this point that older carers may struggle to understand eating disorders within their families. My mother describes her feelings when my daughter Samantha became poorly:

> *I was frightened of the illness because I realized I knew nothing about it and, worse, I couldn't get my head around it to try to begin to understand. In my childhood, what little food we had was there to nourish the body. Surely this eating disorder couldn't have been around then? But yes, I suppose it could after all, because an eating disorder (I now understand) is a mental illness. In our generation we didn't talk about what we couldn't see or didn't understand.*

As my mother's testimony shows, education and communication regarding eating disorders is crucial during all stages of life.

CHAPTER 13

EATING DISORDERS AND SOCIAL NETWORKING

An eating disorder will exploit any cracks in your support strategy among your team of carers. That is why it is so important that the channels of communication are open at all times and that the various carers within a sufferer's life work harmoniously together to provide coherent and consistent support.

Caring effectively for an eating disorder sufferer takes hard work, determination, patience and compassion from everyone concerned. It is, therefore, hugely important to be aware of anything which can infiltrate your support network and potentially undo all your hard-won progress.

The internet is omnipresent in most of our lives. Many of us simply couldn't function without it. At times it can be a valuable source of information. It is, however, often unregulated and should be approached with caution.

The internet can be a valuable source of help and encouragement for sufferers and carers alike, linking them to people enduring similar situations throughout the world and creating a mutually supportive, positive online community. However, the internet's ability to unite like-minded people is both a blessing and a curse.

In 2009, the press conducted a thorough investigation of what were known as 'pro-ana' or 'thinspiration' websites. These websites promote weight loss at any cost. They are set up, run and contributed to solely by people who suffer from severe eating disorders. However, rather than helping one another towards recovery, these sites aim solely to fuel and perpetuate eating disorders.

The people who direct and use pro-ana websites do not see eating disorders as an illness. Rather, they see eating disorder as a positive and aspirational lifestyle choice. They lure vulnerable people into their clutches by claiming to 'understand' the confusing and destructive feelings which categorize the early stages of anorexia. They will then convince sufferers that what they are feeling is natural and healthy, and that the existence of these feelings makes them superior to anyone who is not suffering from anorexia. They will teach users how to fool medical professionals, their friends and family into believing that they are eating. They will share 'tips' on how to promote optimum weight loss. They spread the message that anyone trying to help the sufferer towards recovery is not acting in the sufferer's best interests, and that only they understand the true nature of anorexia and bulimia.

Users will post pictures of themselves in various states of emaciation. Other users will praise them when they have lost weight by writing encouraging comments and urging them to lose yet more weight. Some users will also post comments accusing them of being 'fat' (despite most being dangerously underweight) and tell them that they must try harder. Users will post their daily food intake, measurements, weights and BMIs.

Eating disorders then become a game, with users competing against one another to eat the least, to purge the most effectively, to lose the most weight and to avoid medical intervention for the longest. For every bit of progress you may make in aiding your loved one towards recovery, these sites exist purely to unravel your hard work.

Pro-ana sites can also attract people who are not suffering from eating disorders, but simply searching for genuine weight-loss advice. It is testament to how powerful the appeal of these sites is that they have been shown to actively lure people into eating-disordered behaviour.

While the numerous press pieces in 2009 were a huge step forward in exposing the dangerous and destructive nature of these sites, it also forced them to become subtler and cleverer in their techniques. Make no mistake, despite pro-ana sites now being totally illegal, they still exist. It's just that now they masquerade under the identity of a 'support network' or 'journaling group'.

Owing to the fact that most pro-ana or 'thinspiration' sites claim to be a 'support network', they are very difficult to identify. As a carer, it is therefore of the utmost importance that you are vigilant in spotting whether your loved one might be visiting them. One of the most obvious signs to look out for is the inclusion of photographs on the site. Genuine self-help networks, such as the forums on the Beat or Men Get Eating Disorders Too websites, will not allow users to post pictures of themselves online because these images can be triggering to other users.

The other obvious difference between a genuine support network and a pro-ana site are the inclusion of weights and measurements. All posts on genuine sites are checked by a moderator, who should remove anything referring to how much users weigh, or their daily food intake. This will be stated in their 'users' policy' which can be found on the site itself. Referring to weight or BMI, in particular, is not tolerated by most genuine organizations, because eating disorders are inherently competitive illnesses and users will try to 'out-do' one another.

A discreet sign to look out for is if your loved one suddenly begins to wear a red bracelet. Often, these websites encourage users to wear a red bracelet as a signal to other people within the 'pro-ana' community and, equally, as a reminder not to eat during periods of temptation. Pro-mia (websites which promote bulimia) are far less common, but encourage their users to wear a blue or a purple band.

Social networking sites such as Facebook, Bebo and Twitter should also be handled with caution. While of course these sites do not have any intention of promoting eating disorders, they can present an easy and instantaneous way for sufferers to share potentially damaging information. Eating disorder sufferers will naturally attract other people with the same illness, both in their real and their cyber lives. This can significantly hinder their recovery, because sufferers will 'normalize' their behaviour by surrounding themselves with other people who behave and think in the same way.

The period before sufferers have recognized their illness, or made the decision that they wish to get better, is particularly precarious in terms of the damage potential of pro-ana messages. It is a time during which cyber-relations can have a devastating effect. Like-minded people in the grips of eating disorders can easily reinforce the destructive patterns of thought within the sufferer's mind, renewing their resolve to continue with their dangerous behaviour.

The following are accounts from three young women who are all recovering from anorexia. Each has experienced both the positive and negative aspects of social networking during their illness and as they made their journey to recovery.

Abby

Abby, like many eating disorder sufferers, did not recognize her illness as anorexia in the early stages:

> *I had fallen deep into the pits of anorexia, although at the time I didn't realize it. I thought I was just on a diet but I didn't understand the extremity of what was then my life. I was in search of somebody who would understand what was wrong with me.*

It was at this stage that Abby stumbled upon her first pro-ana website. She describes the people using it as 'kind and friendly – like they cared.' However, they also informed her that she was 'fat' and needed to lose weight. Rather than seeing this for what it was – i.e. potentially fatal advice – Abby took their reaction to her weight as a sign that, 'They were the only people who understood my situation.'

The feedback Abby received from other site users mirrored the contradictory and disordered thinking which categorizes anorexia. While some users praised her weight loss, others would tell her she was fat and 'could do better'. By reflecting and confirming the disordered mind-set of anorexics, pro-ana sites fuel the fire of the disorder, and this is exactly what happened to Abby: 'They made it all seem like a game, and made me further believe that this was my fault, that I was the one in control and that in no way was I suffering from an illness.'

After recognizing the destructive messages being fed to her by pro-ana sites, and starting recovery, Abby also began to notice questionable practices on mainstream social networking sites. She, naturally, befriended other recovering anorexics on Facebook, but believes that some of the information these people post is potentially damaging. She says in particular she is still affected by people 'going on and on about anorexia, or blaming everything in their life on their illness.' She has also had photographs stolen from her Facebook and MySpace profiles and used on 'thinspiration' sites.

The most horrifying aspect of Abby's story, however, is the reaction she has had from current sufferers now that she is in recovery. Anorexia is initially distinguished by feelings of denial, and also by the belief that one can never get better. Because of this, sufferers often misguidedly believe that those who have recovered never had anorexia to begin with. This is, once more, a symptom of the competitive nature of eating disorders, with each sufferer attempting to be the 'best' anorexic or bulimic and to exhibit the most extreme behaviour or lose the most weight. By harbouring the belief that their illness is a life sentence, anorexics believe that they are being the 'best anorexic'.

Abby, who since beginning her recovery has done some volunteering to help other people with eating disorders, says that she has 'received quite a lot of hate online from people claiming I was never ill.'

Luckily, Abby has also formed internet-based friendships with some more positive influences, who have helped her to retain some perspective. She does not, however, consider them as an essential element of her recovery, which is important for carers (and especially parents) to bear in mind when questioning whether sufferers should have access to the internet at all.

Laura

Laura was first lured into using a pro-ana site which claimed to be a 'journaling community'. She was attracted to the idea of being able to freely share her thoughts and feelings during a difficult period of her life, but, like Abby, Laura had no idea she was being dragged into a dangerous online environment.

At first, Laura only read what was being written by other users, rather than contributing herself. The first way in which the pro-ana site negatively influenced Laura was to persuade her not to listen to concerned friends and family. She 'got a sense of validation in my thinking that the people physically around me, my friends and family, were making a fuss about nothing.'

Laura also attributes the influence of the pro-ana site to allowing her to wholeheartedly embrace her eating disorder. Previous to using the site, there had been some doubt in Laura's mind that her behaviour was right. After visiting the site, she 'no longer believed it was a problem.'

Laura then began her own journal (also known as a 'blog'), using it as a place to 'vent about the arguments I had been having with friends and family about my weight and my struggles with food and exercise'. She also began to post entries concerning her weight and food goals.

Other users gave Laura 'tips' on how to lose even more weight. They also convinced her that asking for help was a sign of weakness, and that she should ignore the advice of her carers:

At a time when I was feeling so self-conscious about myself and was struggling so much with the torment going on in my head, having these 'friends' seeming proud of me made me feel accepted. My real, three-dimensional friends were calling NHS Direct in desperation and I was being threatened with being taken out of college by my parents. I felt like the people on these sites were the only ones who actually understood what I was going through. Using pro-ana websites became an addiction and I found myself logging on to them every day.

Unlike Abby, Laura strongly feels that having since discovered a genuinely supportive online community, who are all working towards recovery, has helped her to conquer her illness. She says that her current cyber-community has 'given me hope that it is possible to recover and that I shouldn't give up when faced with a hurdle.'

Laura is also careful to emphasize that pro-recovery online communities can provide a unique form of support which complements that given by other carers:

I found it sometimes easier, when recovering, to speak to people online rather than the people around me. This was not because the people around me weren't supportive, it was purely because I found it easier to speak more openly and honestly with them without feeling like a burden.

Hannah

Ironically, Hannah first discovered pro-ana sites after seeing a television report about them. She describes herself as, 'Intrigued as to what they were'. She then says the sites 'sucked her in.'

Hannah's obsession with pro-ana sites was mainly because of the competitive element of her anorexia. She recalls it as 'a numbers game'. With users posting their daily food intake and exercise regime, as well as their weights, Hannah's illness spiralled out of control. She 'had to eat one calorie less, do one more sit-up, be one inch thinner.'

The site Hannah used to visit now claims to be a support site, and has even issued a statement saying that they will not tolerate any promotion of anorexia within their forums. However, Hannah has visited the site once or twice since recovery to see what progress has been made and the forum is, in her opinion, most definitely still pro-ana.

Like Abby and Laura, Hannah has since found people and organizations online who genuinely wish to help sufferers towards recovery. She believes that finding these sites made her journey back to health 'less of a struggle and certainly less lonely.'

SUMMARY

As a carer, the internet can be your friend or your foe. It is certainly no coincidence that the meteoric rise in eating disorder diagnosis has mirrored the increase in access to the internet. However, the internet is also invaluable in uniting people with a genuine desire to get better and those who can help them on their way.

Hannah's story illustrates the lengths that pro-ana sites will go to in order to disguise their true intentions. The creators and users of these sites are not evil, they are simply so embroiled in their illness themselves that they cannot see anything morally questionable in what they are doing. These sites provide an environment in which sufferers can feed each other's illnesses and affirm each other's misguided beliefs.

The official advice is that pro-ana websites should be reported to Google, who then prevent the site in question from showing up in any internet search. However, many people believe that there is little value in doing this, since the site will simply change its name and URL, or that five more sites will pop up in place of the one which has been removed. Reporting pro-ana websites also forces them to become more subtle and sneaky in their techniques, making them all the harder to distinguish from genuine support forums.

It is, of course, a matter of personal choice whether or not to report a pro-ana site. However, the most important consideration for any carer is to prevent sufferers from using these sites at all. If you do find your loved one visiting a pro-ana site, you should initially have a look at what they have written in the forum or on their blog. It may provide a crucial insight into how they are currently thinking, and allow you to stay one step ahead of their illness.

You then need to turn your attention to preventing them from using the pro-ana site any further. You may choose to introduce them to a genuine forum so they can interact with people who can provide an alternative and healthier way of thinking. You might also opt to apply 'parental controls' to the sufferer's computer, which prevent sites which use certain words from being accessible. You may choose to ban the internet altogether, depending on how old your loved one is and what your relationship is with them.

It is worth remembering, however, that the internet is not an entirely bad influence. There are individuals and organizations online who want to help sufferers towards a healthy future, and their positive influence should not be disregarded. You may find that these sites and internet users contribute to your own network of support, providing ways and means of helping your loved one towards recovery which you are unable to, yourself. Laura's story has shown how this is possible.

As with all elements of effective caring, in this instance, knowledge is power. Simply being aware of the existence of pro-ana sites and being vigilant in checking for signs that your loved one is using them is better than having no knowledge of them at all. I hope that this chapter has given you some insight into the role social networking plays in both helping and hindering eating disorder sufferers. You can find details of pro-recovery online campaigns and forums in the Resources section at the back of this book.

CHAPTER 14

EATING DISORDERS AND THE MEDIA

The portrayal of body image and eating disorders within the media is a veritable minefield (and something which I could probably devote an entire book to, on its own!).

To simplify, I'll explain the most extreme viewpoints. In the red corner we have the people who claim that eating disorders are intensely private, emotionally driven mental illnesses, so it would be irresponsible and patronizing to claim that factors such as our celebrity-worshipping culture, airbrushing and fashion could possibly be at their root. In the blue corner we have those who argue that it is impossible to ignore increasingly unrealistic and artificially enhanced beauty paradigms, and that the immense pressure to conform to these is enough to drive anyone to an eating disorder.

The truth, of course, lies somewhere in between. While there are increased incidents of 'orthorexia' being reported, the vast majority of eating disorders still do not have as their genesis a desire on the part of the sufferer to match up to celebrities and models. However, in many cases the media can provide a catalyst in the creation of body-image issues, as well as providing an obstacle to recovery.

There are also those who argue that eating disorders are a symptom rather than a cause, and that if we weren't put under such immense pressure to match up to impossible beauty ideals, we'd deal with our low self-esteem, or depression, in a different way.

Jess Linley, 22, former Miss England 2010–11, shares her views:

> *Eating disorders are still considered a taboo subject and this needs to be addressed. The glamorization of too-thin models in the media is causing young men and women to become obsessed with their own body image; this, coupled with the over-airbrushing of magazines, gives an unrealistic benchmark that can never be naturally achieved.*

It's important to note, at this stage, that 'the media' represents a great diversity of organizations and individuals, and we must bear in mind all those journalists, television programmes and publications which are working ethically to effect positive change in body image. They do exist. The media, in its entirety, is not the enemy, merely certain sectors of it. The main issues, in terms of eating disorders and body confidence, are advertising, airbrushing and irresponsible body-image reporting. Later in this chapter I will introduce you to some campaigns which are working to effect change in these crucial arenas.

Before this, however, I'd like to share the results of a survey I commissioned, designed to explore the effect of the media on young people. What was revealed is certainly thought-provoking (as well as quite terrifying).

More than 500 young people between the ages of 11 and 19 years old took part. A majority of 57 per cent claimed not to trust what they see, hear or read in the media, and a further 63 per cent believe that the media encourages unhealthy lifestyle choices. However, this does not prevent an overwhelming majority of almost 70 per cent claiming that they have been made to feel bad about their own appearance by something they have seen in the media, and the same percentage have actively attempted to emulate celebrities and models.

At the end of the survey I asked participants to define what beauty meant, to them. Thirty-two of them simply wrote 'thin is good'.

To attempt to gain an insight into the apparent anomalies in the thinking of young people, I interviewed Tom, Ed and Louis, three participants in my survey. Each is 18 years of age and in full-time education. They explained that, while the media may affect each individual to a lesser or greater extent depending on how vulnerable to media messages that person is, those influenced by the media then go on to inflict their views on their peer groups. Ed said this: 'The media affects certain people, then they affect others, for example they feel pressure from their friends.'

We can see from this how any potential damage from the media is magnified, so any research might not be accurately reflecting how influential the media is. The young men also, paradoxically, claimed to be aware of airbrushing and unrealistic imagery within the media, but admitted to attempting to emulate an 'ideal' body type, anyway. This backs up the findings in my survey. The boys say:

> *When you see airbrushed abs, etc. it makes you strive harder. It still plays on your mind, even though you know airbrushing has been used. When I look at images of men on the front of health magazines, with defined, rippled chest and abs, I know that's what I'm aiming for.*

We can see here, worryingly, that images in the media promoting aspirational beauty could, in fact, even be cartoons, and young people would still attempt to emulate them.

It would be remiss to blame celebrities for this. They are at the mercy of their industry, and it's an industry which often demands a warped version of 'perfection'.

Bobby Davro, who has enjoyed a long career in show businesses since the early 1980s, says:

> *I do believe that the pressure to look good within the media can, and has, led to certain celebrities going beyond the normal dieting parameters and this has led, in some cases, to bad health. All celebrities have egos and some are greater than others. Many celebrities become role models to the young and I believe it is their moral responsibility to care about how they look and behave. However, only the media industry can really address this and achieve a fair balance.*

British actress and former anorexic Gemma Oaten says:

> *It was so very difficult for me to go public with my illness. It's a double-edged sword. I want to leave all this behind me and live my life, but then the life I have chosen puts me in the public eye. I can't have it both ways. Acting makes me happy. It's all I have ever wanted to do and it's never been a decision. I hope I am strong enough to deal with the echoes of my past but I will never hide from it.*

Actress Mikyla Dodd echoes this:

> *The media plays a huge part in projecting images of how people should look, and yet the images are seldom untouched by a computer. The pictures of people with no make-up on, having a normal day and wearing baggy clothes are portrayed as negative, rather than just normal. There is so much pressure on society to be glamorous and a perception that beauty is in some way connected to being slim or, worse still, super-skinny.*

We can see from this, as well as the stories of Steve Blacknell and John Stapleton in Chapter 8, that celebrities are aware of the situation at hand and the impact that they have. However, on the other hand their careers and livelihoods depend on looking a certain way. It is the industry which needs to rethink and reform, rather than the celebrities themselves. Let's now take a look at some important campaigns which are working within the media, fashion and beauty industries to ensure these changes are made. You can find details of how you can learn more about and support these campaigns in the Resources section at the back of this book.

THE DOVE CAMPAIGN FOR REAL BEAUTY

In 2004 Dove launched a series of adverts and online videos, questioning the prevailing beauty aesthetic. Using models who were older, larger or of a different shape or race than the public are accustomed to seeing, they hoped to subvert the detrimental effect more traditional advertisements have had on the self-esteem of, in particular, British women. This was dubbed 'the Dove Campaign for Real Beauty' and gave rise to the subsequent Dove Self-Esteem Fund programme.

There can be little doubt that this was a well-timed commercial decision, with the campaign being well received by a society who were increasingly aware of the narrow beauty ideals being presented to them. A Dove survey reveals that, in the past five years, the number of women who would like to see 'real' models used in advertising has risen from 74 per cent to an astronomical 95 per cent. It's little wonder, then, that the Dove Self-Esteem Fund became a household name and the Dove brand has been inextricably linked with positive body image ever since its inception.

The controversy, however, arises during discussions of whether more inclusive beauty paradigms have any effect on eating disorders. In the red corner, we have many advertising executives and medical professionals who claim that eating disorders are an intensely private and emotionally driven illness, born out of traumatic experiences. They would therefore argue that to place the blame at the foot of the media (which the Dove campaign, indirectly, seems to) is both irresponsible and wilfully misunderstanding the issues at hand. In the blue corner, there are an army of ex- and current sufferers who can testify to the negative impact of the use of unrealistically slender and very young models, from first-hand experience.

The truth lies somewhere in between. Whilst eating disorders are, as we have already discovered, unique to each sufferer, there can be little doubt that the media and advertising can fuel the fire of low self-esteem, and perpetuate potentially dangerous feelings of low self-worth.

As Susan Ringwood of Beat observes, 'Building positive self-esteem would make a difference to everyone, including those who have eating disorders.' She remarks that Beat ambassadors, who have all had personal experiences of eating disorders, tend to opine that advertising 'didn't cause it … but it was part of the picture.' It also, she asserts, 'makes it really hard for [them] to get better.'

Erin O'Connor, a model who has made contributions to the Dove Campaign for Real Beauty, is vocal about the age issue also: 'We see girls of 13 and 14 on the catwalk, and that has a real impact on grown women.' Few would argue that, with anorexia especially, part of the problem is girls refusing to relinquish their youth. Many anorexics fear developing into a woman and all the adult pressures they associate with this. Using models who are not yet fully developed is bound to exacerbate this issue.

Susan Ringwood is aware that discussion of the beauty and fashion industries is often not as high as it perhaps should be on the political and social agenda: 'The [issue] is still seen as rather trivial [but] the eating disorder side of it is really serious.'

Susie Orbach, a pioneering psychologist and writer, and one of the first people to highlight the link between body image and feminism with her seminal work *Fat is a Feminist Issue* (first published in 1978), has been involved with the Dove Campaign for Real Beauty since the start. Yet, although she was responsible for overseeing many of the advertisements, she still speaks of how surprised she was the first time she saw a Dove billboard, because the images used jarred so poignantly with the norm.

As Sandra, a woman who has had what she describes as a 'brief flirtation' with bulimia, says:

> *I'm as much an advocate for feeling good about yourself as the next woman, but when I first saw the Dove adverts my initial response was, 'Who wants to see a fat girl in her underwear?' I know it's wrong, and it just goes to show how influenced I am by traditional advertising.*

When asked what she believes is the solution to self-esteem-bashing advertising, Susie Orbach says simply, 'There is no motivation for advertisers to change [if we keep buying their products].'

Perhaps the greatest impact Dove have had is through their online marketing. 'Dove Evolution' is a video (available on YouTube) which shows the extent to which models are airbrushed – a model is digitally retouched so that her neck is longer, her eyes further apart, her skin suspiciously flawless and her overall appearance several years younger. As the film closes, a line of text reads, 'No wonder our perception of beauty is distorted'.

In a world where this, unfortunately, continues to be the case, the Dove Campaign for Real Beauty is a welcome breath of fresh air.

(NB: The quotations from this section were taken from a round-table discussion with Jo Swinson MP, Erin O'Connor, Susie Orbach and Susan Ringwood as well as a Dove executive. You can view this discussion in its entirety at www.dove.co.uk.)

CAMPAIGN FOR BODY CONFIDENCE

The Campaign for Body Confidence was founded by two British MPs, Jo Swinson and Lynne Featherstone, in 2010 (although it has no specific political dimension).

The group enables discussion on body-image issues, as well as influencing necessary change within the field. Jo Swinson works with a number of Britain's most influential body-image campaigners including Susie Orbach, All Walks Beyond the Catwalk, the Centre for Appearance Research, the YMCA, Girlguiding, Professor Janet Treasure, Body Gossip and even me!

To date, the Campaign for Body Confidence has been most successful in its endeavours to have extreme airbrushing either banned, or clearly labelled. In 2010, an advert featuring middle-aged supermodel Twiggy for Olay's 'Definity' eye illuminator was removed because of pressure from the campaign (it was ridiculously airbrushed, particularly around her eyes, which were entirely wrinkle-free). In 2011, similar cosmetics advertisements featuring Julia Roberts and Christy Turlington suffered the same fate.

Jo Swinson is keen to emphasize that, although the campaign can call for extreme airbrushing to be removed, it is ultimately pressure from the public which will make advertisers change their attitudes dramatically and permanently.

The campaign also undertakes research, takes steps to implement body confidence in the media, and works within education to encourage a wider range of physical activities within schools. By placing the emphasis on fitness rather than aesthetics, it is hoped that people should appreciate their bodies for what they are capable of, rather than how they look.

When it comes to eating disorders, Jo Swinson says that they are 'patronisingly perceived' within the media – they tend to be presented as a problem suffered only by girls in their teens, and to be hugely over-simplified. We will explore this later in the chapter.

ALL WALKS BEYOND THE CATWALK

All Walks was founded by respected fashion guru and television presenter Caryn Franklin, internationally recognized model Erin O'Connor and PR and marketing expert Debra Bourne. These three hugely influential women joined forces to make pioneering changes within the fashion industry, in an attempt to reverse some of the detrimental effects of super-slender and very young beauty ideals.

Caryn Franklin says:

We wanted to create imagery that would become iconic to celebrate a broader range of body and beauty ideals ... Because there is so much post-production work on imagery now (and social networking and new media can broadcast this very effectively), young women are exposed to more and more images of unachievable beauty. It normalizes the look of very thin models and makes it seem as though it is commonplace, when in fact it is not.

All Walks have catapulted larger, older and more ethnically diverse models into the spotlight, to showcase a broad range of beauty ideals. They work predominantly in London, but the effect of the stir they have created (within the media and at events) has reverberated within all the world's main fashion capitals.

There can be little doubt that existing in a world in which unhealthily slender and unrealistic images – assaulting the eyes from every computer and television screen, billboard and magazine – has a detrimental effect on those suffering from eating disorders. Whether or not one agrees that the fashion industries create eating disorders is a matter of personal opinion. However, the work of All Walks in demonstrating that beauty comes in many guises is a hugely positive influence in helping sufferers towards recovery.

By promoting uniqueness, diversity and health as beautiful and iconic, All Walks is encouraging the public, both sufferers and non-sufferers alike, to accept themselves.

BODY GOSSIP

Body Gossip invites the public to write something about their body and to submit it to them via their website. A selection of these pieces is then performed by a cast of well-known actors, models and musicians, either in live theatre events or short films (which can be viewed on their YouTube channel). They are also publishing a Body Gossip book featuring a wide range of stories from the public and celebrities alike.

The idea behind the campaign is to give real people a powerful platform to express their feelings and opinions on body image. Ruth Rogers, the campaign's founder, says:

> Body Gossip is for the people in the middle, the real people who are so often swept under the carpet. It's an opportunity for them to say 'Hey! This is me! This is what I'm going through!' It's also an opportunity for the public and celebrities to stand shoulder-to-shoulder. So often, they are presented as divided on body-image issues, but the truth is we're all facing the same pressures and we all have a responsibility and a need to address them.

While the Body Gossip stories vary in topic (from adolescence to ageing, disability, sports, illness, injury, tattoos and piercings, pregnancy, etc.), the majority of the pieces the campaign receives are written by past and present eating disorder sufferers. Their flagship film *This One Is for You* is an inspiring tale of eating disorder recovery, which is viewed every day on YouTube by some sufferers to help give them the strength to fight their illness. Ruth says:

One person's story has the potential to help and inspire so many. Not only are we reassuring the public that, whatever they are facing, they aren't alone, but we're getting a unique glimpse into what's really going on with the problem of body image in this country.

EATING DISORDERS IN THE MEDIA

Of course, the issue is not merely the role the media plays within eating disorders, but also the role eating disorders play within the media.

Within this book I have made reference to the 'standard' eating disorder story which sometimes can be told in the press:

- The case study will be about a past or present sufferer of anorexia (as opposed to one of the many other eating disorders).
- The case study subject will have reached a weight under 6 stone.
- The subject will be a girl between the ages of 14 and 25.
- The story will include numerous references to weight and BMI.
- The story will list a typical day's diet while the person was ill.
- The story will include 'shocking' revelations relating to how the person suffered.

- The magazine or television programme will show images of the sufferer at their lowest weight.

- The story will present the issue as a nutritional problem, as opposed to a mental health problem.

- The story will perpetuate the idea that eating disorders are a life sentence.

These stories can be damaging in many ways, some of which we have explored throughout this book. Usually the subject of the case study has the best intentions, wishing to use their experiences to raise awareness and to provide hope, but their stories can be mishandled. It's not even straightforward enough to place the blame on journalists, because they are themselves at the mercy of editorial processes and somewhat misguided beliefs as to what the public want to read. The main problem with eating disorder reporting is that it is concerned solely with the 'hows' of eating disorders and very rarely with the 'whys'.

THE SUCCEED FOUNDATION

The Succeed Foundation is working to change that. They are an organization concerned exclusively with researching and promoting a greater understanding of eating disorders.

Founded in 2010 by Karine Berthou, the Succeed Foundation differs from many charities that have been set up in the sector. They are dedicated to tackling the root causes of eating disorders, challenging stereotypes and mentalities, and offering a shared voice. Their aim is to facilitate diagnosis at the earliest possible stage by introducing both established and cutting-edge programmes, up-to-date research and new technologies to halve the average recovery time of someone suffering from an eating disorder. They disseminate the information via the most effective support channels to those who can benefit from their research, such as medical professionals, carers and sufferers alike. Their work helps to educate and raise awareness about the need for change.

In March 2011, the Succeed Foundation released the results of some powerful research, undertaken in partnership with the University of the West of England, Bristol. It is worth noting both the positive influence that the work of the Succeed Foundation has had on eating disorder reporting, and the willingness of the media to release their findings to the public.

My family are proud to be ambassadors for the Succeed Foundation. We support their work and are passionate about bringing their research to the attention of the public. You can find more details about the Succeed Foundation in the Resources section at the back of this book.

SUMMARY

We have seen throughout this chapter the crucial role the media has to play, both in fuelling and in reporting eating disorders.

Eleni Renton (director of Leni's Models), sums up the changes which need to be made when she says:

The media distorts what the average person thinks they should look like. We are no longer seeing this just with models, but with Hollywood celebrities and reality television stars. Ultimately, the most important thing should be for fashion, and all of the media, to portray health.

We are led to believe that the media is all-powerful, and that we have no control over the images and ideals we are fed by it. However, ultimately the media is a commercial enterprise and gives the public what it believes it wants. As members of the public, we have the ability to effect change, by not buying or watching the media products which offend us or which we understand to be potentially damaging. We can also support the groups mentioned in this chapter, who work tirelessly at wrestling with the media to make it more responsible, in the hope that we will all eventually benefit.

There are many complex arguments within the media debate. However, the research done within this field shows that the public do wish to see a change in beauty paradigms.

The media is also a powerful tool which could potentially be used to promote a better understanding of eating disorders. The difficulty lies in the fact that with such a visual medium, the emphasis is on weights, BMIs and shocking 'poorly pictures'. For anyone reading this who works in television or publishing, I urge you to turn your creative brain to thinking of a different way to report on eating disorders. It is so crucial that the general public understand that eating disorders are an illness of the mind which can affect anyone, regardless of age, race, gender or social background.

AFTERWORD

I would like to think that this book has lived up to its title and has given you the strength, motivation and, above all, the *hope* you need as a carer to continue your journey successfully.

When I started writing this book two years ago, it was very much a hobby. Over time, as my understanding and knowledge developed, I began to realize how much a book like this was needed for carers of people with eating disorders. I certainly would have benefited from the support and information within these pages, especially when I faced the kinds of challenges you may now be experiencing.

In creating this book I have met many wonderful people from all walks of life, who have believed in me enough to share their thoughts and experiences; in turn I have shared them with you. Through them I have gained an even greater understanding of and insight into the world of eating disorders and the effect they have not only on the sufferers but on their friends, family, loved ones and carers as well.

As I have reiterated throughout this book, and as many of my case studies attest, my message to you has to be that you must never give up hope. Eating disorders can be beaten, and families and relationships rebuilt.

In closing, I will leave you with my guiding principle:

'The cure is in the recovery, there is no elevator; you have to take the stairs.'

RESOURCES

CHARITIES

Beat
Helpline: 0845 634 1414
www.b-eat.co.uk

Beat is the UK's leading eating disorder charity and the largest of its kind in the world supporting people affected by eating disorders and campaigning on their behalf. It runs telephone helplines, local support groups and a website with information, message boards and online chat. Last year the charity had direct contact with 250,000 individuals, and many, many thousands more through its website and the media.

Registered Charity Number: 801343

Men Get Eating Disorders Too
Helpline: 0845 634 1414
www.mengetedstoo.co.uk
sam@mengetedstoo.co.uk

MGEDT is a national charitable organization that is dedicated to raising awareness and supporting the needs of men with eating disorders. Their website provides essential information that is specific to the needs of male sufferers and is an online platform on which men can get their voices heard by telling their stories and exchanging peer support in the online forum and live chat sessions.

Beyond the website, MGEDT reaches out to sufferers, carers and the general public in a number of engagement platforms whether these are via social media and blogs, outreach in the community and in the press/media. They also provide essential training to professionals working in the field.

Registered Charity Number: 1139351

S.E.E.D (Support and Education for Eating Disorders)
Tel: 0844 391 5539
lancashireseed.btck.co.uk
www.facebook.com/groups/SEEDPreston
Twitter: @SEED_Breathe
prestoneds@hotmail.co.uk

S.E.E.D is a Beat-affiliated, local and accessible charity based in Preston, Lancashire providing a network of support for individuals suffering eating distress and their carers/families/partners or friends, offering information, advice, education, resources and practical help. Weekly drop-in service, fortnightly support groups and fortnightly carer advice and information clinics are accessible through an annual membership fee of £10.

Registered Charity Number: 1144313

S.E.E.D. (Support and Empathy for people with Eating Disorders)
Tel: 01482 718 130
www.seedeatingdisorders.org.uk
info@seedeatingdisorders.org.uk

S.E.E.D. Eating Disorders Support Services is a Beat-affiliated group operating in Hull, East Yorkshire, made up of ordinary people who have had first-hand experience of eating disorders in one form or another and feel it is important to share experiences with others and help in any way possible. They know from personal experiences how difficult it is to obtain the professional help and assistance in overcoming eating disorders. Marg Oaten MBE is the charity's secretary.

Registered Charity Number: 1108405

The Succeed Foundation

Tel: 020 7052 9203
www.succeed-foundation.org
office@succeed-foundation.org

Based in Kensington, London, the Succeed Foundation is committed to supporting and developing innovative and evidence-based programmes and strategies to prevent and treat eating disorders and promote well-being. Founded in 2010 by Karine Berthou, the Succeed Foundation is focused on making available these strategies to men, women and children, young and old, whatever their profession or situation.

Current strategies include:

- UK National Fat Talk Free Week, October 2012
- Succeed Body Image Programme in schools and universities across the UK
- New technologies to support individuals with eating disorders and their carers

Together with individuals, carers, clinicians and researchers, the Succeed Foundation is working towards creating a world free from eating disorders.

Registered Charity Number: 1136289

Young Minds

Parents' helpline: 0808 802 5544
www.youngminds.org.uk
www.vik.org.uk

The voice of young people's mental health and well-being, providing advice, information and training for young people, parents and carers and professionals, and campaign to raise awareness about the importance of good mental health and to challenge stigma.

Registered Charity Number: 1016968

CAMPAIGNS AND ORGANIZATIONS

All Walks Beyond the Catwalk
Tel: 0207 289 6230
www.allwalks.org
info@allwalks.org

Body Gossip
www.bodygossip.org
www.facebook.com/bodygossip
www.youtube.com/bodygossip
Twitter: @_BodyGossip
info@bodygossip.org

Campaign for Body Confidence
www.campaignforbodyconfidence.org.uk
www.facebook.com/campaignforbodyconfidence
Twitter: @body_confidence; @joswinson
jo.swinson.mp@parliament.uk

Dove
www.dove.co.uk

Self-esteem resources available from Dove.co.uk: Self-Esteem Workshop Guide for teachers, Activity Guide for Youth Leaders, Discussion Guide and Activity Guide for Mums and Daughters.

Hungry for Change
hungryforchange@hotmail.co.uk
www.hungryforchangeofficial.com

CONTRIBUTORS HAPPY TO BE CONTACTED

Ester Akinnuwa
estherakin@yahoo.co.uk

Juan Arroyo
Tel: 07867 594961
jarroyo@aol.com

Abby Baker
littleorangeturtle@hotmail.co.uk

Steve Blacknell
teeheesb@yahoo.com
www.steveblacknell.com

Kered Clement
www.complexd.co.uk

Complexd is the UK's first online lifestyle magazine celebrating multicultural women of all shades, shapes and sizes.

Carolyne Cross (Isis Beauty Academy)
Tel: 01932 232 322
info@isisbeautyacademy.co.uk
www.isisbeautyacademy.co.uk

Suzanne Dando
www.suzannedando.com

Russell Delderfield (Eating Disorders in UK Men)
University of Bradford
Tel: 01274 236 794
www.bradford.ac.uk/eating-disorders-and-men

Laura Forbes (BodyTalk)
Tel: 07799 691555

Tony Ford Counselling
Tel: 0788 148 8048
www.tonyfordcounselling.co.uk

Alison Fuller (Holistic Therapist)
Tel: 07811 123494
info@serenehealing.co.uk
www.serenehealing.co.uk

Ian Graham
For further information on TFT or to obtain practitioner contact details, please go to www.thoughtfieldtherapy.co.uk or the British Thought Field Therapy Association website (www.btfta.org)

Lori Henry
www.lorihenry.ca
Twitter: @lorihenry

Author of *Silent Screams* (Lulu.com, 2008), a book of poetry about bulimia

Hinchley Wood School
Claygate Lane
Hinchley Wood
Surrey KT10 0AQ
info@hinchleywood.surrey.sch.uk

Max Kirsten C.Ht.
Tel. 0800 0286367
info@maxkirsten.com
www.maxkirsten.com

Jenny Langley
www.boyanorexia.com
jenny@boyanorexia.com

Boys Get Anorexia Too (Paul Chapman Publishing, 2006)

Leni's Model Agency
info@lenismodels.com
www.lenismodels.com

Jess Linley
jess.linley@hotmail.com
www.jessicalinley.com
Twitter: @jesslinley

Kyra Mathers (BodyTalk)
Tel: 07515 530 541
www.kyramathers.com

Debbie Roche (NotEDuk)

www.noteduk.com

No to Eating Disorders UK primarily provides information, advice and support to young people and their carers.

Martin and Marion Shirran

Tel: (34) 951 311 591
www.gmband.com
mail@gmband.com

The developers and trademark owners of the Gastric mind Band treatment worldwide, Martin and Marion are based at the Elite Clinic in Malaga, Spain.

Ian Sockett

ian.sockett@virgin.net

Nicki Waterman

Personal Trainer
nickiwaterman.com

Rebecca Whitford

Yoga Instructor
rebeccawhitford.com
rebeccawhitford@googlemail.com

Books (with Martina Selway): *Little Yoga* (Hutchinson, 2005) and *Sleepy Little Yoga* (Hutchinson; 2007)

FURTHER SOURCES OF SUPPORT AND TRAINING

Breathe (Eating Disorder Treatment Service)
Tel: 0844 391 5539
www.breathe-therapy.co.uk
www.fulwoodtherapycentre.co.uk
www.facebook.com/BreatheEDS
help@breathe-therapy.co.uk
Twitter: @SEED_Breathe

Breathe is a not-for-profit social enterprise providing a local and accessible research-based multi-disciplinary treatment programme for all types of eating distress utilizing specialist therapists at their Fulwood Therapy Centre in Preston, Lancashire. Breathe provide individualized treatment packages – one-to-one or group therapy – aiming to provide a challenging but positive journey experience towards emotional and physical well-being.

Mikyla Dodd
Mikyla Dodd released her own fitness and nutrition DVD *The Lose Weight Workout* and published her self-penned autobiography *Playing the Fat Girl* (Hodder, 2007).

Kevin Laye
kevinlaye.co.uk

Harley-Street-based therapy practitioner and corporate coach; international trainer and public speaker; co-founder of the Meta Changework Practitioner Association (MCPA).

Models of Diversity
www.models of diversity.org

Models of Diversity campaigns for more diversity in models, and demands that the fashion and marketing industries recognize the beauty in women of all races, ages, shapes, sizes and abilities. Their mission is to change the face of fashion and modelling.

SupportLine
Helpline: 01708 765 200
www.supportline.org.uk

SupportLine provides emotional support, advice and information to children, young people and adults throughout the country by telephone, email and post on a variety of issues including eating disorders, low self-esteem, depression, abuse.

Professor Janet Treasure PhD FRCP FRCPsych
Professor Treasure has written several books on the subject of eating disorders:

Anorexia Nervosa: A Survival Guide for Families, Friends and Sufferers (Psychology Press, 1997)

– with Ulrike Schmidt: *Getting Better Bit(e) by Bit(e): Survival Kit for Sufferers of Bulimia Nervosa and Binge Eating Disorders* (Routledge, 1993)

– with Gráinne Smith and Anna Crane: *Skills-based Learning for Caring for a Loved One with an Eating Disorder: The New Maudsley Method* (Routledge, 2007)

ABOUT THE AUTHOR

 **Lynn Crilly** lives in Surrey with her husband Kevin and their twin daughters, Charlotte and Samantha. Through using her unique and very effective form of counselling she has now established herself as one of the country's leading private therapists, working with people from all walks of life, ages and genders. She is admired for her passion and understanding – something she attributes to the strength and loyalty of her family and friends, with whom she spends as much time as possible.

www.lynncrilly.co.uk

We hope you enjoyed this Hay House book.
If you would like to receive a free catalogue featuring additional
Hay House books and products, or if you would like information
about the Hay Foundation, please contact:

Hay House UK Ltd
292B Kensal Road • London W10 5BE
Tel: (44) 20 8962 1230; Fax: (44) 20 8962 1239
www.hayhouse.co.uk

***

Published and distributed in the United States of America by:
Hay House, Inc. • PO Box 5100 • Carlsbad, CA 92018-5100
Tel: (1) 760 431 7695 or (1) 800 654 5126;
Fax: (1) 760 431 6948 or (1) 800 650 5115
www.hayhouse.com

***

Published and distributed in Australia by:
Hay House Australia Ltd • 18/36 Ralph Street • Alexandria, NSW 2015
Tel: (61) 2 9669 4299, Fax: (61) 2 9669 4144
www.hayhouse.com.au

***

Published and distributed in the Republic of South Africa by:
Hay House SA (Pty) Ltd • PO Box 990 • Witkoppen 2068
Tel/Fax: (27) 11 467 8904
www.hayhouse.co.za

***

Published and distributed in India by:
Hay House Publishers India • Muskaan Complex • Plot No.3
B-2• Vasant Kunj • New Delhi - 110 070
Tel: (91) 11 41761620; Fax: (91) 11 41761630
www.hayhouse.co.in

***

Distributed in Canada by:
Raincoast • 9050 Shaughnessy St • Vancouver, BC V6P 6E5
Tel: (1) 604 323 7100
Fax: (1) 604 323 2600

***

Sign up via the Hay House UK website to receive the Hay House
online newsletter and stay informed about what's going on with your
favourite authors. You'll receive bimonthly announcements
about discounts and offers, special events, product highlights,
free excerpts, giveaways, and more!
www.hayhouse.co.uk

JOIN THE HAY HOUSE FAMILY

As the leading self-help, mind, body and spirit publisher in the UK, we'd like to welcome you to our family so that you can enjoy all the benefits our website has to offer.

EXTRACTS from a selection of your favourite author titles

COMPETITIONS, PRIZES & SPECIAL OFFERS Win extracts, money off, downloads and so much more

LISTEN to a range of radio interviews and our latest audio publications

CELEBRATE YOUR BIRTHDAY An inspiring gift will be sent your way

LATEST NEWS Keep up with the latest news from and about our authors

ATTEND OUR AUTHOR EVENTS Be the first to hear about our author events

iPHONE APPS Download your favourite app for your iPhone

HAY HOUSE INFORMATION Ask us anything, all enquiries answered

join us online at **www.hayhouse.co.uk**

292B Kensal Road, London W10 5BE
T: 020 8962 1230 E: info@hayhouse.co.uk